SEDE VACANTE

THE LIFE AND LEGACY OF ARCHBISHOP THỤC

EDWARD JARVIS

Apocryphile Press
1700 Shattuck Ave #81
Berkeley, CA 94709
www.apocryphilepress.com

Copyright © 2018 by Edward Jarvis
Printed in the United States of America
ISBN 978-1-949643-02-2 | paperback
ISBN 978-1-949643-03-9 | epub

Please join our mailing list at
www.apocryphilepress.com/free
We'll keep you up-to-date on all our new releases,
and we'll also send you a FREE BOOK.
Visit us today!

Contents

PREFACE

This is the strange story of Archbishop Pierre Martin Ngô-dinh-Thục. His career can be divided into two parts: he was initially quite successful, becoming only the third ever Vietnamese Roman Catholic bishop. But Archbishop Thục was part of the extraordinary and controversial ruling family of Vietnam, the Ngôs, and his destiny was inevitably bound up with that of his brothers' regime — which ended in bloody disaster, literally. Thục attended the Second Vatican Council in Rome but was prohibited from returning to his — by that time war-torn — homeland. The second part of his life was, in Thục's own words, made up of "failures. Providential failures."[1] He became involved, mysteriously and unexpectedly, with the bizarre Palmarian religious cult, something he later regretted. He then became involved with the ultra-traditionalist Catholic counter-reform movement — which can sometimes be almost as bizarre as the Palmarian cult — and Thục did not seem to regret this as much. In between these two endeavors he became involved with a series of other characters and sects who could be called, yes, you guessed it, bizarre. Thục's various escapades earned him at least two excommunications. These are the bare bones of the story.

It has been pointed out that hardly anyone seems to want to get the story of Archbishop Ngô-dinh-Thục straight. Traditionalist Catholics either canonize him as a heroic and "spiritually sovereign prelate"[2] who fought to save the Church from error with his personal brand of "combative Catholicism,"[3] or dismiss him as "an old fool who lacked enough presence of mind to confer a valid sacrament."[4] Neither assessment is accurate. These are typically the polarized positions of those with a vested interest in the Catholic traditionalist or counter-reform movement, particularly where the matter of the so-called 'Thục bishops' is concerned —

unofficial or unauthorized bishops who trace their ordinations (or 'consecrations') back to Archbishop Thục. Even Thục's detractors often find it more convenient to simply ignore his more reckless and embarrassing exploits, such as his involvement with the Palmarian sect, and Thục's career in Vietnam as a key part of the brutal Ngô regime tends to be glossed over. But it is possible to make other assessments of Pierre Martin Ngô-dinh-Thục, and his strange behavior does not completely defy explanation.

There is, of course, every possibility that Thục was severely psychologically affected by the dramatic events of his life: that this well-qualified, high-ranking bishop was driven to unsound, rebellious behavior after suddenly being bereaved, exiled, impoverished, and marginalized. The Church abandoned him, it may have appeared, and he took revenge. It is certainly likely that Thuc was angry with the Church he had dedicated his life to. He might have expected more from it — to raise more of an objection to the massacre of the Ngôs, to take a stronger stance in favor of Vietnamese Catholics, to facilitate Thục's return to his homeland. But Thục had dedicated his life to other things too — advancing his brothers' political careers, influencing foreign policy, establishing his own economic powerbases and defending the Ngô family regime to the bitter end. Thục had been a powerful man. It can be difficult for modern Western and European Catholics to really imagine a truly powerful bishop, upon whose words local government officials hang, whose orders the police and army obey, whose requests for donations are instantly and fearfully met. Thục had been accustomed to stomping around demanding his own way and getting it. All of these are aspects of Thục's former life, which he was suddenly forced to give up, and his weird and pathetic behavior in later life may not have been so random and impulsive after all — it may have been just a protracted attempt to claw back some power and influence.

It is useful to try to get a clear picture of the world Thục was born into and lived in; fortunately, the story of Christianity in Southeast Asia is a fascinating topic in its own right. Early proponents of

Christianity in Southeast Asia tended to dismiss the local religions as 'idolatry' and 'animism,' but in time it became clear that Christianity could only achieve a foothold when viewed through, and in harmony with, established local beliefs. This may sound radical or even like syncretism or polytheism, but in fact this was already a familiar and well-established phenomenon. In Western societies, all religions tend to be evaluated and discussed using Christian terms such as congregation, worship, and ministry, and according to Christian concepts such as revelation, discipleship, and salvation etc. etc.[5] In the same way, popular forms of the major world religions in Southeast Asia are only ever perceived through a locally-produced lens.[6] Christianity is therefore never found in its 'pure' form, and it "does not compete with other religions but complements them."[7]

Often motivated by religious principles, the colonized peoples of Southeast Asia eventually began to show their mettle. In World War Two they played a full part in defeating the Japanese, and this brought forward the expectation that they would subsequently be rid of their colonial occupiers too — the British in Burma and Malaya, the Dutch in the East Indies, and the French in Laos, Cambodia, and Vietnam. Religiously speaking, this aspiration gradually began to find expression in a theological shift — Southeast Asian Christianity, for example, went from being a theology of domination, imported by the colonial masters, to a theology of liberation.[8] The former, wrote the Indian Jesuit Aloysius Pieris, had "resulted from the unholy alliance between Christian missions and Western colonialism."[9] Its purpose had been to instill a Christian moral worldview to sit alongside the European economic and social worldview. By the time of Vietnam's empowering defeat of the US, local theology was discussed in terms of both 'liberation theology' and 'third world theology'.

Archbishop Pierre Martin Ngô-dinh-Thục's life spanned all of these events. He lived for 87 years and 2 months. He was born in 1897 (like Paul VI) in the French Protectorate of Annam (like Ho-chi-Minh); Thuc was Annamese and Vietnamese; he died in the USA in 1984. He also spent periods living in Italy and France. Thục's story is told here in eight chapters: the Making of a Bishop; the Making of a Regime; the Making of a Catastrophe; the Making of a Revolution; the Making of a Farce; the Making of a Movement; the Making of a Dignified Exit. Then, the final chapter discusses the theological issues arising from the story, with some concluding clarifications and the dispelling of some lingering Thục myths.

In discussing the legacy of Archbishop Ngô-dinh-Thục, a Catholic 'new religious movement' (NRM) called *sedevacantism* features heavily. Sedevacantism is considered to be the 'extreme' end of traditionalist Catholicism,[10] and it deserves to be discussed both in relation to the story of Ngô-dinh-Thục and in its own right. It has been observed that sedevacantism may be the only Catholic NRM to be homegrown in the USA; another example could be the Catholic Worker Movement, the diametrical opposite of sedevacantism! Though it is now fair to call it a movement, sedevacantism started life as a discreetly-held 'theological position' which circulated long before it was baptized sedevacantism. Fr. Anthony Cekada, a prominent sedevacantist writer and broadcaster, explained that sedevacantism emerges from a realization that the reforms of the Second Vatican Council subverted and corrupted the Catholic Church. Sedevacantists believe "that the New Mass is evil and the new doctrines are errors. Evil and error can come only from non-Catholics [as popes] — not true Successors of Peter who possess authority from Jesus Christ."[11] This leads sedevacantists to the conclusion that there has not been a true 'successor of Peter,' a true pope, since 1958 — whence the term sedevacantism, from the Latin phrase *sede vacante,* meaning 'as the [Holy] See is vacant'. It may be loosely translated as 'the chair of Peter is vacant' — there is currently no pope.

There have always been periods of *sede vacante* of course, between the death of one pope and the election of another. *Poste Vaticane* even prepares a range of postage stamps proclaiming '*Sede Vacante,*' to be issued during the *interregnum* period. The contention of the sedevacantists is that we are currently in a very long period of *interregnum* and that there has not been a true pope for sixty years. It is difficult to estimate the number of sedevacantists, for several reasons. At least a few sedevacantist sympathizers may have seen it as being in their interests to exaggerate their numbers. At the same time it is likely that not all those who are effectively sedevacantists would identify themselves as such.

It remains extremely rare for a serving priest of the Catholic Church to 'turn' sedevacantist; no bishop has ever tried to lead his diocese into sedevacantism, though among both priests and bishops there may very well be sedevacantist sympathizers or even closet sedevacantists. Archbishop Marcel Lefebvre made statements leaning heavily towards sedevacantism, but only one serving bishop has ever publicly and unequivocally declared his allegiance to sedevacantism — Pierre Martin Ngô-dinh-Thục.

Most writing about sedevacantism has so far been intentionally or unintentionally polemical, especially within the pro- and anti-sedevacantist camps. In fact, both the source and audience for most writing on the topic are sedevacantism's supporters and detractors themselves. Non-partisan writing about sedevacantism, such little as there is, tends to run the risk of dismissing it, ridiculing it or underestimating it. This may be unwise, considering that although sedevacantism may be an extreme, the approach, style and orientation of the pope have the power to alienate and disenfranchise vast numbers of Catholics. In light of all this, it seems judicious to outline my own position on, and experiences of, sedevacantism and traditionalist Catholicism. Basic reactions to sedevacantism could be grouped in three categories: a) pro-sedevacantism, b) anti-sedevacantism, and c) no very strong opinion either way. Perhaps the majority of both Catholics and non-Catholics will have no very strong opinion, largely because they are not always well-informed about it. Some Catholics will lump sedevacantists together with the 'Latin Mass brigade' and consider them all fanatics. Other Catholics may consider the whole topic disturbing, distasteful, or just not important enough to dwell on. But mainstream Catholics will also be found wavering on the edges of all three opinion groups; plenty of conservative mainstream Catholics are sympathetic to some of the sedevacantists' arguments. It is a common sedevacantist argument that many conservative and traditionalist Catholics are close to sedevacantism — acknowledging the heresy of Vatican II and the errors of recent popes — without 'taking the leap' and drawing what sedevacantists see as the logical conclusion. I myself am neither for nor against sedevacantism, and I am neither indifferent nor uninformed. I am confident in having maintained a concerned impartiality on the subject. But I would not want impartiality to imply a cold and detached approach; I do not propose to offer a forensic vivisection of sedevacantism, or reams of data and papal pronouncements. I do propose to assess and evaluate according to Catholic theology and historical evidence.

The case of Archbishop Thục can elicit strong feelings, as does sedevacantism, and this book takes a warts 'n' all approach. It is neither an attack on Thục and sedevacantism, nor an apologia for Thục and sedevacantism. This has caused me to reflect on the rules of unbiased writing: if several — or all — good sources agree on something, report it; if one good source says it, then it needs further investigation and comparison with other sources. If two good sources disagree with each other, report both. In all cases, emergent facts have to be placed back into their social, cultural and historical context, which is the challenge facing the author. Ultimately it is the reader who decides; the unbiased author carefully lays out the evidence, in full context, but does not judge. This is without prejudice to the fact that there may, perhaps, be a legitimate place for biased writing on the subject, but this book is no hagiography and I have no vested interest in the subject.

In terms of sources about Archbishop Thục, he himself penned an autobiographical essay (in French) around 1976, which was published in the German-based *Einsicht* magazine in 1982. Some other aspects of the Ngô-dinh-Thục story are fairly well documented: the events of Palmar de Troya and the Palmarian sect have produced a good range of studies and reports; the best contemporary sources are all in Spanish, while the best current research is by Magnus

Lundberg at Uppsala University. There is a good body of work about conservative Catholicism, and to a lesser extent the traditionalist Catholic movement (as opposed to conservative mainstream Catholicism — they are not the same thing). Various essays are in circulation addressing the debates around the 'Thục bishops' — the unofficial bishops who derive their powers from Thuc — and the contingent theological and sacramental issues. There is of course a very substantial body of work about Thục's brother, Ngô-dinh-Diêm, and Vietnam-US relations. All of these topics necessarily include and involve Archbishop Thục.

But this is the first time that Archbishop Thục takes center stage in a full-length book. Thuc's autobiographical essay is still an important and enlightening source, but it suffers from several defects: it cuts off in 1975, unfortunately, and it is predictably unreliable; it absolutely must be studied in conjunction with other, independent sources in order to glean the full, unbiased story. All the translations from French, Spanish, Italian, and Latin used here are my own, with one or two small exceptions. Archival material about Archbishop Thục, also rather predictably, is scarce — the Vietnamese Catholic Church has been through vast upheavals: coups, occupations, and two wars – each one a decade long – which ravaged Vietnam, in addition to the five years of World War Two and much guerilla fighting in between; a total of thirty-five years of war, 1940-1975. After each upheaval and with every hostile State measure in between, the Church has had to reinvent itself countless times, each time with less and less room and fewer resources for preserving the memory of people like Archbishop Thục. Today, in spite of serious problems, the Church in Vietnam is in many senses freer and less persecuted than at any time in the last 50 years; there is little interest in clouding this new dawn with the ghosts of the Ngô years. But archival research is always worthwhile and always sheds some light on the subject at hand. Thanks are therefore due to the Catholic Bishops' Conference of Vietnam, the Archdioceses of Huế and Ho-chi-Minh City, and the Diocese of Vinh Long, as well as the Maryknoll archives in New York.

11

There has always been a great deal of interest in the origins of the Vietnam War and consequently in the Ngô family regime. It is truly an incredible story — this time seen through different eyes, with the older brother Thục as the protagonist. The temptation to make Shakespearean comparisons is strong, though there are film noire and vaudevillian elements to the story as well. If Lady Macbeth were to join the Corleone family the cast may nearly be complete, especially if there were room for a Spanish (Palmarian) Abbott and Costello as well. This is not to say that any of the people involved in the story are ridiculous or absurd; as in any human drama there are merely individuals caught up in complex historical moments, situations not entirely of their making, and subject to countless factors outside of their control. The individuals in this story who have sought to find strategies to cope with critical situations, for the greater good, are naturally entitled to respect. Those who have acted with other, sometimes difficult to identify priorities, can at least expect that the circumstances be described fairly and accurately — after that, judgment is someone else's job.

In the preface to my first book, *God, Land and Freedom: the true story of I.C.A.B.*,[12] I contrasted the career of Bishop Carlos Duarte Costa with that of Archbishop Marcel Lefebvre; I stated that Duarte Costa should not be considered a 'Latin American Lefebvre'. Similarly, it would be a mistake to cast Archbishop Thục as a 'Vietnamese Lefebvre'. In the case of Duarte Costa and Lefebvre, the differences were primarily about political orientation, not theology; between Thục and Lefebvre the differences are reversed. In spite of how he may be recast by posterity, Archbishop Thục was in many ways profoundly theologically progressive, in harmony with his anticolonial third-world theology roots. His Asian Catholicism verged on syncretism. But Thục and Lefebvre did not differ politically. Lefebvre was deeply devoted to the far right; Yves Congar called it a "uniform spirit running through his writings and his actions."[13] He denounced democracy and praised genocidal regimes.[14] Thục too was deeply committed to authoritarian politics, Ngô family style; unelected rule, control through fear, personality cult of the leader, and abduction and torture of opponents. But the Ngôs went beyond typical right-wing oppression, which often does at least adhere to its own declared value system; the Ngôs ran roughshod over their own ostensible Catholic ideals, indulging in extortion, racketeering, fraud, currency manipulation, and murder. More than once it has occurred to me that the story of the Ngôs would have been excellent subject matter for the late Mario Puzo.

The Godfather brings me to a brief mention of my own introduction to sedevacantism and traditionalist Catholicism. I can thank Don Angelo, my Godfather, for first telling me about these matters. I remember very clearly the moment I first heard about sedevacantism. It was seventeen years ago when I was a student in the pontifical university system in Italy. I was living in a spectacular place called the Sanctuary of Santa Maria della Palomba, where Don Angelo, a priest of the Archdiocese, was Rector. I wish I had taken notes when he explained sedevacantism to me. "So, are the *lefebvriani* sedevacantists too?" I asked. "Not exactly... well, effectively...." Within a few months of that conversation (we had no idea at the time) Don Angelo and I were to be spending our days in the company of one of the most famous sedevacantists, if not *the* most famous sedevacantist, in the world. Here is how it came about:

On more than one occasion, student filmmakers were drawn by the beauty of that ancient Sanctuary — commonly called 'La Palomba' — to film there, so when Don Angelo informed me one day that another group was coming to town to shoot a film, I just shrugged. "But I'm going to need your help with them; they're English," he said — Don Angelo does not speak English — "and they want me to be involved somehow... I'm not sure what they want; one of them is coming to talk after Mass...". Well, as it turned out, they were American, not English (in Italy 'English' gets used as an umbrella term for all English speakers), and it was no student film that they were coming to make, it was Mel Gibson's *The Passion of the Christ* (during production it was still called 'The Passion,' and Mel Gibson was still adamant that there should be no subtitles). The person coming to talk after Mass was Jim Caviezel, and Don Angelo's role was to be that of on-set priest, closely supporting Jim as a kind of spiritual adviser, with me as interpreter and assistant to the Don.

Mel Gibson is one of a small number of people worldwide who were actually raised as sedevacantists rather than discovering sedevacantism in adult life. Sedevacantist households do certainly exist, but the vast majority of adult sedevacantists follow a path typically from mainstream conservative Catholicism, via the Latin Mass, via increasingly uncompromising doctrinal positions, before finally arriving at the conclusion of *sede vacante*. My involvement in *The Passion* was an extraordinary and wonderful experience, being present throughout the most intense and dramatic moments of filming. It also definitely fueled my interest in Catholic traditionalism. I spent some time on set talking to Abbé Michel de Bourges, an elderly French priest brought in by Mel Gibson — because, I believe, none of the local priests knew how to celebrate the Tridentine Mass. The Abbé belonged to the Institute of Christ the King, a traditionalist order within the official Catholic Church. My interest progressed to visiting the Institute's extremely beautiful seminary in Tuscany, which was a fine immersion in the traditional Latin liturgy. I have continued to monitor and study the traditionalist movement since then.

For those readers less interested in the liturgical, theological and sacramental issues arising from the story of Archbishop Thục — the 'Church politics' as it were — I am confident that they will find as wide a range of fascinating topics as I have. This story involves the history and culture of Southeast Asia, and their clashes and crossovers with the European and American Christian mindsets; it touches on the huge topics of religion and politics, Church and State, the background to the Vietnam War, and new religious movements (NRMs) and sects. At the story's heart are conflicts: true faith and / or religious freedom, unity and / or diversity, and the sources of and evolution of what being Catholic actually means. This unusual tale is well supplied with historical curiosities and exciting events — it could be considered both entertaining and weird. The history of the twentieth century is itself endlessly entertaining and fascinating, with its intertwining of huge national and international events, its extremes of politics and clashing ideologies, and the intrigues and interplay of religions and governments in fast-developing new moral realities; I am pleased to say that all these elements and more are to be found in *Sede Vacante: The Life and Legacy of Archbishop Thục.*

Edward Jarvis
Rangoon, Burma
9th October 2018

Notes

1   Ngô-dinh-Thục, "'Misericordias Domini in Aeternum Cantabo'": Autobiographie de Mgr. Pierre Martin Ngô-dinh-Thục, Archeveque de Huế' [sic], *Einsicht* (Special Edition), Una-Voce-Gruppe Maria, Munich, August 1982, p 79

2   *Einsicht,* No. 6, Year 14, February 1985, Una-Voce-Gruppe, Munich, p 153

3   Ngô-dinh-Thục, op. cit. 1982, p 12

4   Anthony Cekada, 'The Validity of the Thuc Consecrations,' [published in Spanish as 'La Validez de las Consagraciones de Monsenor Ngô-dinh-Thục'], *Revista Integrismo,* Buenos Aires, 2006, p 4 – http://www.traditionalmass.org/articles/article.php?id=60&catname=13 [accessed 12th June 2018]

5   Cf. Janet Alison Hoskins, 'An Unjealous God? Christian Elements in a Vietnamese Syncretistic Religion,' *Current Anthropology,* Vol. 55, No. S10, 1st December 2014 (volume supplement), p S302

6   Cf. Aloysius Pieris, 'Political Theologies in Asia,' Ch. 18 in Peter Scott and William T. Cavanaugh (Eds), *The Blackwell Companion to Political Theology,* Blackwell, Oxford, 2004, [pp 256-270], p 258

7   Aloysius Pieris, op. cit. p 262

8   Cf. Aloysius Pieris, op. cit. p 256

9   Ibid.

10 Cf. Joseph A. Komonchak, 'Interpreting the Council – Catholic Attitudes toward Vatican II,' in Mary Jo Weaver and R. Scott Appleby (eds), *Being Right – Conservative Catholics in America,* Indiana University Press, Bloomington IN, 1995, [pp 17-36] p 26

11 Anthony Cekada, 'Resisting the Pope, Sedevacantism and Frankenchurch: a short case for sedevacantism' 2005, p 12 – http://www.traditionalmass.org/images/articles/Resist-Franken-P.pdf [accessed 6th June 2018], also published in *The Remnant,* November 2005

12 Cf. Edward Jarvis, *God, Land & Freedom: The True Story of I.C.A.B.,* Apocryphile Press, Berkeley CA, 2018

13 Yves Congar, *Challenge to the Church: The Case of Archbishop Lefebvre [La Crise dans l'Eglise et Mgr Lefebvre],* Collins Liturgical Publications, London, 1977, pp 46-47

14 Cf. Yves Congar, op. cit. p 16

I

CAPITULUM PRIMUM

'CONFUCIAN AND CATHOLIC'[1] —
THE MAKING OF A BISHOP

More than one hundred years ago in Vietnam, Ngô-dinh-Khâ, Archbishop Ngô-dinh-Thục's father, used to tell his children this story:

Once there was a rich man who had two servants. One of the servants was his favorite, while the other servant had made a mistake and fallen out of favor with his master. The rich man plotted to dispose quietly of this inept servant. He called the baker and said 'I will send one of my servants to you with a message: when a servant comes to you carrying a message from me, take hold of him and throw him into your lime oven.' As it was in his interest to win favor with the rich man, the baker agreed.

The next day the rich man sent the unfortunate servant off to the baker with a note. On the way into town, the servant heard the bell ringing in church where Mass was about to start. He suddenly remembered what his parents had taught him: 'Whenever you get the chance to go to Mass, go,' so he decided to take a detour and went to attend Mass.

The rich man was agitated, anxious to know that his plan had been carried out. 'Go to the baker,' he ordered his favorite servant, 'and ask him, "have you done as I asked?"' The favorite servant hurried off to the baker, and announced 'I have a message from my master...' — upon which the baker took hold of him and threw him into the oven.[2]

Ngô-dinh-Khâ, who never missed daily Mass himself, told this story in order to instill the same lifelong commitment in his children. He always took them with him to church, and those who had already made their First Communion would join their father in approaching the altar and kneeling to receive the Eucharist. Prayers and Rosaries book-ended each day in a devoutly Catholic Vietnamese family more than one hundred years ago. The Ngôs inhabited the region called Annam, the central region of three — north, center, and south — that make up modern-day Vietnam. In antiquity, Thục wrote,

"the Viet people occupied the region that is now called Peking (Beijing), through which the great Yellow River flows. The Chinese encroached into this very fertile land where the Vietnamese earned a comfortable living. Against the vast numbers of invaders, the infinitely less numerous Viet started a fatally unequal battle and lost. But the Viet did not cease to resist — even as they were pushed to the south — their last capital city in present-day Chinese territory being Canton (Guangzhou).[3]

"When Canton was occupied by the 'heavenly ones' [the Chinese], the Viet people found an area conducive to defense, which was named the Gates of Annam because it blocked the path of the Chinese. The Chinese later succeeded in breaching the gates and occupying the Yellow River Delta upon which Hanoi was built — and that for almost a thousand years. The Viet never lost courage and finally succeeded in expelling the Chinese."[4]

In the early nineteenth century, France helped the Nguyên royal family to unite the three regions now known as Vietnam — Tonkin in the north, Annam in the center, and Cochin-China in the south — under a united Empire, named after the central province of Annam. The capital of Annam was the imperial city of Huế, Thục's birthplace. In exchange for their help, the French obtained increasing concessions until they were able to create a 'protectorate'

18

including Laos and Cambodia, and on 17th October 1887 'French Indochina' came into being.[5]

French Indochina was almost exactly ten years old when Ngô-dinh-Thục was born. Thục's birth, coincidentally, came shortly after the arrival of another major player in our story; while Thục would be called Peter, the other boy would eventually be called Paul. Nobody could have foreseen that the baby boy who came into the world on Sunday 26th September 1897 would become one of the most controversial figures in modern Catholicism. He was destined to be a driving force behind reforms that would transform the Catholic Church, though it was claimed that the reforms were rooted in ancient traditions, thus earning criticism from both conservatives and progressives. His period of governance would bridge the old and the new age, and would lead some to question the very authenticity of his being pope. He was named Giovanni Battista Enrico Antonio Maria Montini and he would become known as Paul VI. He was born in Concesio, Brescia province, Italy. In faraway Huế, Vietnam, the other boy, Ngô-dinh-Thục, was born just ten days after Montini. The two babies, Montini and Thục, already had several things in common: both their fathers were prominent laymen who were involved in politics and the Church; they both had brothers who would grow up to be active in politics; both Montini and Thục would go to minor seminary, they were both destined for lives dedicated to the Church, and they would both gain doctorates in Canon Law. Both Montini and Thục, arguably, would harbor ambitions for the Papacy, though of course not both would achieve them. Ngô-dinh-Thục, given the French baptismal names Pierre Martin, was born in Huế on Wednesday, 6th October 1897. "I am a Ngô," he wrote seventy-nine years later;

"Ngô is one of the family names in Vietnam. I believe that I am not mistaken when I say that the number of Viêt family names does not exceed one hundred. The name with the most descendants is Nguyên, with the most prolific branch being the royal family. The one with the least family members is mine. According to legend, the Ngôs are the descendants of the first native royal family in an

19

independent Vietnam. Perhaps this explains our patriotism and devotion to our country a little. Beyond the legend of our royal descent, no other Ngô was conspicuous in Vietnam's history until the brilliant, yet tragic, appearance of my family."[6]

The Ngôs were widely considered an "aristocratic, old family,"[7] but Thục's 'legend of royal descent' was just that, a legend. The Ngôs tended to propagate the idea, especially among westerners, that their ancestors had been mandarins as far back as the sixteenth century, but as American reporters later uncovered, "while [Ngô-dinh-Khâ] was a court chamberlain and a high-ranking adviser to Emperor Thanh Thai in Huế, his grandfather was only a fisherman-peasant, not a scholar."[8] The Ngô family had converted to Catholicism back in the seventeenth century, when the French Jesuits first landed. In the nineteenth century, the Ngôs had suffered violent persecution at the hands of renegade Buddhist mobs.[9] The persecution of Catholics provided a pretext for increased French 'protection' of Indochina. There can be little doubt that this family history contributed to the Ngôs' later hostility toward Buddhists, as well as their on-off affinity with the French colonialists. Ngô-dinh-Khâ, Thục's father, lost his entire family in anti-Catholic riots, but survived because he was in Malaya studying for the priesthood. He returned to Huế in order to rebuild the family. He passed the mandarinate exams, became fluent in French, and entered the civil service, rising to become court chamberlain to the Nguyên royal dynasty. Khâ's first wife died soon after the wedding, but his second wife bore him twelve children over the course of twenty-three years. The first, Khôi, was born around 1891. He would grow up to be tall and handsome, and also quite outspoken and impetuous. He would follow his father in becoming a mandarin and an influential court figure. The young Khôi soon had siblings — a sister and two brothers, though the two boys died in early infancy. This created a gap between the children which, along with Thục's later absences from home, resulted in Khôi as the eldest remaining somewhat detached from the other brothers.[10] Thục himself would enjoy a much closer relationship with his younger brothers. Ngô-thi-Giao, the elder sister, would eventually have four daughters, who all became nuns. Thục was the fifth child in total, and third surviving child. He was regarded as bright but not the most religious of the children. He entered the minor seminary in An Ninh at the age of 12 and would spend eight years there before going on to study philosophy at the major seminary in Huế. Another brother was born after Thục, who also died in infancy. The next surviving Ngô brother, Ngô-dình-Diệm, was born on 3rd January 1901, three years and two months after Thục. Diệm was shy and the most devout of all the children. He was destined to become the most successful and prominent of the brothers; even his childhood games had a seriousness and intensity that seemed to presage the Vietnam of later decades. Thục later recalled that Diệm

"amused himself by coercing my two little sisters and my two little brothers into 'playing war.' First, he drew moustaches above their lips with a piece of charred cork, and the rifles were made from the central stalks of large banana leaves. It was comical. But for Diệm it was quite serious, and he led this army consisting of two little soldiers and two little soldierettes, stamping the ground with their bare feet: *Un-deux, Un-deux.* Woe betide any distracted soldier: a sabre blow on the derriere called him or her back into line."[11]

Thục would later echo Diệm's 'mini-militarization' of the Ngô children in his motto as a bishop: *Miles Christi* — Soldier of Christ. Diệm attended the French lycée and became engrossed in French history, language and literature. But he was already wary of France's tradition of revolutionary philosophies — his father, showing incredible foresight, warned him to stay away from Nguyễn-sinh-Cung, another youth growing up in Huế, who would later be known as Ho-chi-Minh.[12] When Thục was 18 his younger brother Diệm, aged 15, joined him in pursuing minor seminary studies. But Diệm was not cut out for the priesthood in Thục's opinion and he encouraged Diệm to change his mind. Thục claimed that Diệm tried out for the novitiate of the Brothers of the Christian Schools but could not stay because of an aversion to eating fish.[13] The thoughts of a young man being released from seminary might

21

be expected to turn toward forbidden pleasures and pursuits which are suddenly no longer forbidden — not so Ngô-dinh-Diệm. He promptly took a lifelong vow of celibacy, and shunned movies, dancing, gambling, magazines, and entertainment in general — there would only be work and prayer from now on. Diệm studied for the civil service and rose steadily through the ranks during the 1920's.[14] He was widely known as a devout Catholic and an early and articulate anti-Communist.[15]

After Diệm came a sister, Hiệp, the favorite of the family (and one of the garden-game soldierettes); she would act as nurse-maid to the subsequent children. Then came another sister, Hoáng, the other soldierette (less beloved than Hiêp, one senses) who married an entrepreneur and whose daughter would marry a minister in the Ngô regime. Years later, the favorite sister Hiệp's son, Nguyễn-văn-Thuận, would become the second priest of the family, eventually rising to Cardinal and, as of 2018, heading towards beatification.

What about the rest of Diệm's sibling army, with the burnt-cork moustaches and banana-leaf stalk rifles? In the Ngôs' future regime, these little soldiers would have more than banana-stalk rifles to conduct their war games with. The next of the little soldier siblings, Nhu, was born on 7th October 1910. Ngô-dình-Nhu was "a born intriguer. He delighted in spending vast amounts of time and energy to trick people into doing the simplest and most normal tasks,"[16] according to the war reporter David Halberstam. He was apparently "arrogant, vain … [and] a little contemptuous of Diệm, whom he considered to be his intellectual inferior."[17] The other little boy soldier was Ngô-dình-Cẩn, born around 1912. He was the most practical, most traditional, and most homely of the Ngô children. In later life he was considered the least westernized brother — he rarely left Huế and never once traveled abroad.[18] But Cẩn was as sharp as the others — a shrewd and unscrupulous merchant of cinnamon, rice and opium,[19] who became the unofficial feudal overlord of Huế and the entire central region of Vietnam; a racketeer and dictator, according to some. The last brother, Luyen, was born in 1914, an impressive 23 years after his eldest brother

Khôi. Luyen, the baby, would go on to become the playboy of the family, whose behavior was distasteful to his ascetic brother Diệm. Luyen was sent to study in France as a child, and was destined for a career in the diplomatic corps. The Ngô family was held together by what Thục called "combative Catholicism."[20]

"The weekday schedule was always the same. In the morning, wake up at six to the sound of the bells of Phû-cam Cathedral, our parish. The boys and girls stormed into the kitchen to wash themselves and to put on our knee-length habits (our ceremonial outfits) and followed father to Holy Mass. The children all kneeled beside him. Our father participated with closed eyes and hands clasped together but always ready to shake the boys if they appeared distracted. Father went to the Lord's Table daily, accompanied by the children who had received First Communion. He was practically never absent from daily Mass, even on stormy days."[21]

Even in the face of some anti-Catholic backlash, the European missionaries had clearly done a good job of implanting Christianity in Southeast Asia. In its most aggressive form, colonial Christianity tended to dismiss local religions as 'polytheism' and 'idolatry,' while western anthropologists began to refer to them more diplomatically as 'animism' or 'nature worship.' In the twentieth century the word 'cosmic' gradually came to be used not just as an umbrella term for local tribal and clannic belief systems, but also to describe the local forms taken by the major world religions in the Southeast Asian region.[22] The cosmic religious outlook views all the forces of nature as personal divine beings working alongside humans, and upon death all are absorbed into the cosmos together. The forces of the natural world are not instruments in the hands of people but their co-workers, jointly participating in the marvel of existence. This results in a widespread cultural appreciation of worldly things being sacred, and of the sacred being something of this world — a "sacred this-worldliness."[23] This is thought to explain the long tradition of active participation in revolutionary and independence struggles by clannic and tribal peoples throughout Asian history.[24] There is no cultural equivalent of the western maxim that religion and politics do not mix, because there is no equivalent of the western philosophical dividing line between the worldly and the sacred. This disparity became evident with the arrival of the first Christian missionaries in Southeast Asia, especially considering that the prevalent European ideal during the same period was that religion belongs "in the apolitical realm of values and ideals."[25]

Families like the Ngôs were proof of the missionaries' success in transplanting Christianity from its European setting, but according to the Jesuit Aloysius Pieris, western religions "are never found in their 'pure' form because, when they spread in various parts of Asia, they had to sink their roots always in a cosmic culture as the only natural soil available."[26] What can be found instead are popular and cosmic forms of what could be called the metacosmic religions such as Christianity, but also Islam in other parts of the continent. These local forms are "not rejected as deviations but appreciated as a cosmic expression, or, more precisely, the cosmic base, of these metacosmic religions."[27] Even the Ngô brothers, reflecting on their upbringing, described it as both "Confucian and Catholic."[28] During his ministry Thục defended local interpretations of Catholicism and promoted local influence over it.[29] In later years he lamented Catholicism's tendency toward "the leveling of all particularities inherent in every civilization,"[30] calling it "abuse of power."[31] This was the Việt spirit, the Việt patriotism which Thục attributed to his (supposed) royal ancestry. The Ngôs were Catholic but still "Việt through and through. From a Christian perspective, we are obedient to the Roman Church ... we accept unanimity in dogmas of faith, but alongside diversity in areas that do not concern dogma."[32]

Thục, however, did not have a lot to say about the dialogue between religion and politics, which would become so important in his history and the history of his family. But it was not an innovation of the Ngôs that religion and politics should be dimensions of each other. The establishment of Catholicism in Southeast Asia was at least partially politically motivated, or at least its facilitation by the ruling powers was. Furthermore, the presence and persecution of Catholics in Vietnam had served as a pretext for the creeping colonization of what became French Indochina. As in many colonized regions of the world, religion was effectively hijacked to serve political ends. Asian Christianity in general has manifested two strictly political theological outlooks: from the middle of the second millennium the prevailing theological vision could be termed a 'theology of domination,' in contrast with the 'theology of liberation,' which appeared and took hold in the closing decades of that same second millennium.[33] "The former was implicitly operative in the policy of *Euro-ecclesiastical expansionism* which resulted from the unholy alliance between Christian missions and Western colonialism."[34] The European colonizers of Southeast Asia invariably gave high priority to the religious dimension as the primary way of importing their social, cultural and moral values, alongside their economic, civil, and military ones. This reflected the European ideal of Christendom, with society as "an organic whole, governed by two parallel and universal powers — the Pope and the Prince."[35] Fusion with local ways and beliefs was not generally considered an impediment to the spread of Christian values; rather it was regarded as something to be utilized. What results is a kind of "*symbiosis* of religions"[36] rather than the one religion overtaking the other; "Christianity does not compete with other religions [in Asia] but complements them."[37]

This harmony is reflected in the geopolitical sphere with the popularization of the 'third world' understanding, though the idea is perceived without negative connotations and not in the pejorative sense of 'third place.' Especially in Francophone regions like Vietnam, 'third world' is faithful to the original French meaning of *tiers monde*, indicating an *alternative world* to be aspired to; a third way of doing things. Nations such as Vietnam embraced this thinking, having experienced one way, namely colonial domination and military occupation, and facing a potential second way, namely becoming a satellite state of a superpower, or an outpost of economic imperialism. The decolonizing nations of the 1950's and 1960's, whether in Africa, Asia, or the Mediterranean, aspired in reality to become adjuncts of neither one world bloc nor the other.

25

This sense of 'third world' as *tiers monde* also corresponds to the Greek Fathers of the Church when they applied the same word *triton (genos)* to Christianity; this was in order to emphasize that their religion was neither a Judaic nor a Hellenistic religion but a *tertium quid,* a 'third something.'[38] The third world concept was found to coherently reflect people's experiences to such a degree that it easily crossed from geo-politics to religion, and 'third-world theology' emerged.

Thanks in part to their complex and hybrid family faith, the Ngôs constituted a formidable family unit, convinced of their self-righteousness.[39] Though they themselves would not have doubted that their Catholicism was as pure as it could be, it was a form of Catholicism that allowed for diversity; it facilitated cohabitation with other customs and traditions — the Ngôs were as much Confucian and Mandarin in their lifestyle, outlook, habits, and values, as they were Catholic. They would apparently see no incompatibility with their outward behavior later in life. Their particular brand of "combative Catholicism,"[40] as Thục called it, with the family as ruling party, would ultimately be their downfall, as would their clan loyalty; their interdependence was such that each one became impervious to outside advice or help, and when one Ngô fell they all fell. "In late 1963, when American officials in Vietnam were discussing what type of man would be the best alternative to Diệm, one of them was asked about a candidate's necessary qualities. 'Well, first of all he should be an only child,' he said."[41]

Thục's family life during his seminary years consisted of just two long summer months at home, and no occasional visits. Longer absences were to come with his period of studies in Rome and Paris. Thục was ordained to the priesthood on 20th December 1925 and was sent to complete his theological education in Rome, where he studied at the Pontifical Gregorian University, precisely at the time of its transfer to the current location in Piazza Pilotta. Construction on the current building had begun in 1924, on a site chosen for its proximity to the Pontifical Biblical Institute, which had opened in 1909. This was the culmination of the Gregorian's rebuilding after the seizure of its property by the revolutionary government in 1870. During Thục's studies the university was based at the Palazzo Gabrielli-Borromeo. The new building was finally completed in 1930. Thục was said to have achieved no fewer than three doctorates, in Philosophy, Theology, and Canon Law, though it seems that the Gregorian archives cannot confirm this. Thục completed his education with a term at the Sorbonne, where he lectured for a time. While in Paris he also completed teaching qualifications at the Catholic University of Paris. It may seem like an incredibly full educational portfolio, but it was a sign of the times; there was no reason to believe that Thục would ever get another chance to visit Europe for further studies. He was an asset in the making, an able priest, and every skill he brought back from Europe moved the Church in Vietnam a step closer to autonomy. Thục returned to Vietnam in 1927, and the following year his sister Hiệp gave birth to a son, Nguyễn-van-Thuận, the future Cardinal, who would go on to attend An-Ninh seminary as his uncle Thục had done. Thục was appointed professor at the College of the Vietnamese Brothers in Huế, and then a professor at the major seminary, also in Huế. Subsequently he became a professor and then Dean of the *École de la Providence Divine,* the College of the Divine Providence. Thục was doing very well, and the future was promising. The rise to prominence of all of the Ngô brothers was about to begin. But history would lead them down paths which they could not have imagined, even in a fairy story:

> Once there was a rich man who had two servants. One of the servants was his favorite, while the other servant had made a mistake and fallen out of favor with his master. The rich man plotted to dispose quietly of this inept servant.

The ancient Vietnamese tale, often recited to the Ngô children, has a certain biblical ring to it. But how well does it correspond to the real-life characters of the Ngô story? Who would play the part of the rich man, who shows his great benevolence to one servant while condemning the other to death for a trifle? He evidently considers himself judge and jury, assuming power over life and death:

> He called the baker and said 'I will send one of my servants to you with a message: when a servant comes to you carrying a message from me, take hold of him and throw him into your lime oven.'

Does one of the Ngô brothers resemble the favorite servant, who does nothing wrong but is cast into the flames thanks to a misunderstanding? Could one of them be the well-meaning but inept servant who makes a mistake and falls foul of his boss — and would his simple piety save him in real life?

> As it was in his interest to win favor with the rich man, the baker agreed.

Perhaps one Ngô brother would be like the baker, who did not set out to do evil, but found it in his best interests to go along with the plots and schemes of others. Ngô-dinh-Khâ told his children this story hoping to instill in them the virtue of keeping the Faith above all else — but it may tell us a lot more about the Ngô family's somewhat unforgiving outlook on the world, and the fine line they would walk between triumph and disaster. Khâ could not have known that the tale presaged the trials and tribulations to come in his children's lives, but fact can sometimes be stranger than fiction.

Notes

[1]   James S. Olson and Randy Roberts, *Where the Domino Fell: America and Vietnam 1945 to 1990,* St. Martin's Press, New York, 1991, p 55
[2]   Cf. Ngô-dinh-Thục, "'Misericordias Domini in Aeternum Cantabo': Autobiographie de Mgr. Pierre Martin Ngô-Dinh-Thục, Archeveque de Huế" [sic], *Einsicht* (Special Edition), Una Voce-Gruppe Maria, Munich, August 1982, p 16
[3]   Ngô-dinh-Thục, op. cit. p 7
[4]   Idem p 8
[5]   Cf. Hilaire du Berrier, *Background to Betrayal: The Tragedy of Vietnam,* Western Islands, Belmont MA, 1965, pp vii-viii
[6]   Ngô-dinh-Thục, op. cit. p 13

[7] David Halberstam, *The Making of a Quagmire,* Random House, New York, 1965, p 40

[8] Robert Shaplen in the *New York Times,* 14th May 1972, p 16 — "[Contrary] to what [Diệm] told many Westerners, including myself in a six-hour conversation I had with him in 1962, his ancestors were not mandarins as far back as the 16th century. This was what he apparently wanted Westerners to believe, but Vietnamese who are descended from the succession of imperial rulers of Vietnam have assured me that, while Diệm's father was a court chamberlain and a high-ranking adviser to Emperor Thanh Thai in Hue, his grandfather was only a fisherman-peasant, not a scholar."

[9] Cf. James S. Olson and Randy Roberts, op. cit. p 55

[10] Cf. Ngô-dinh-Thuc, op. cit. p 18

[11] Idem p 20

[12] Cf. James S. Olson and Randy Roberts, op. cit. p 55

[13] Cf. Ngô-dinh-Thục, op. cit. pp 16-17

[14] Cf. James S. Olson and Randy Roberts, op. cit. p 55

[15] David Halberstam, op. cit. p 40

[16] Idem p 50

[17] Idem pp 50-51

[18] Cf. David Halberstam, op. cit. p 206

[19] Cf. James S. Olson and Randy Roberts, op. cit. p 99

[20] Ngô-dinh-Thục, op. cit. p 12

[21] Idem pp 15-16

[22] Cf. Aloysius Pieris, 'Political Theologies in Asia,' Ch. 18 in Peter Scott and William T. Cavanaugh (eds), *The Blackwell Companion to Political Theology,* Blackwell, Oxford, 2004, [pp 256-270] p 258

[23] Idem p 259

[24] Cf. Aloysius Pieris, op. cit. p 259

[25] Daniel M. Bell Jr., 'State and Civil Society,' Ch 29 in Peter Scott and William T. Cavanaugh (Eds), *The Blackwell Companion to Political Theology,* Blackwell, Oxford, 2004, [pp 423-438], p 430

[26] Aloysius Pieris, op. cit. p 259

[27] Idem pp 259-260

[28] James S. Olson and Randy Roberts, op. cit. p 55

[29] Cf. Charles Keith, *Catholic Vietnam: a Church from Empire to Nation,* University of California Press, Berkeley CA, 2012, p 177

[30] Ngô-dinh-Thục, op. cit. p 9

[31] Idem pp 9-10

[32] Idem p 9

[33] Cf. Aloysius Pieris, op. cit. p 256

[34] Aloysius Pieris, op. cit. p 256

[35] Daniel M. Bell Jr., op. cit. p 425
[36] Aloysius Pieris, op. cit. p 263
[37] Idem pp 261-262
[38] Cf. Aloysius Pieris, op. cit. pp 256-257
[39] Cf. David Halberstam, op. cit. pp 55-56
[40] Ngô-dinh-Thục, op. cit. p 12
[41] David Halberstam, op. cit. p 50

II

CAPITULUM SECUNDUM

'BUILT WITH THEIR SWEAT AND FERTILIZED WITH THEIR BLOOD'[1] — THE MAKING OF A REGIME

In January 1938, at the age of 40, Father Ngô-đinh-Thục was chosen by the Vatican to lead the Apostolic Vicariate of Vinh Long in the Mekong Delta. He was consecrated bishop on 4th May 1938, being only the third Vietnamese priest ever to be raised to the rank of bishop. Priests, it is fair to note, are not obliged by Canon Law to accept the challenge of being promoted to bishop. Refusals are not uncommon and some priests refuse two or three nominations before accepting the role. Often, before accepting promotion to bishop, a priest will request time to pray, celebrate a Mass, or meditate before the Blessed Sacrament. Thục, bravely, did not hesitate to accept, though he was surely aware that he was not receiving an easy or glamorous posting. Vinh Long was a new, non-urban vicariate, an embryonic diocese — a "no-man's land"[2] — which had been carved out of the larger Saigon vicariate (formerly called the West Cochin-China vicariate). Thục was a priest of the central region of Annam, the heartland of royalty, culture and erudition, which he said provided Vietnam with all its governors and revolutionaries.[3] Three of the first four Vietnamese Catholic bishops hailed from the central region, including Thục of course. He was a native of the imperial city, born into an aristocratic family, or so he wanted to believe. And here he was, destined to minister in the demanding south, where he would have to work hard to prove his worth.

The southern region may not have had the fame for culture and scholarship of the central region, but it had the privilege of being directly under French rule; it was not merely a 'protectorate' like the rest of Vietnam. Southerners were granted French citizenship, and their lands were also blessed with rich and fertile paddy fields. Those from further north were considered *bân* — meaning junk-trading people or 'boat traders.' Thục was to be a sort of foreign missionary bishop in his own country. Forty years later he took pride in the fact that in its choice for "the first native bishop [of Vinh Long] the Holy See looked favorably upon a 'bân,' a 'boat-trader's son.'"[4] But Thục saw a lot more significance in his appointment than that. In his consecration homily his first thanks went to Rome — his "spiritual and intellectual homeland"[5] — and he then thanked Pope Pius XI, and the Propaganda Fide offices. After that, however, he had stark words for the European missionaries, especially MEP (*Société des Missions Étrangères de Paris*) to whom he made it clear that their days of lording it over the Vietnamese were finished. For Thục, this was the implicit meaning of Rome's nomination of a third Vietnamese bishop. Having built the Catholic Church in Vietnam "with their sweat and fertilized [it] with their blood,"[6] the European missionaries of MEP were now prevailed upon to cede control of the local Church to the Vatican, who in turn placed it directly into the hands of the Vietnamese people. Bishop Thục reinforced this message in his first pastoral letter, making it clear that under his leadership Vietnamese priests, with their "holiness, intellect, and education,"[7] would be given the prime positions in the diocese, with the rapid phasing-out of the European missionaries. Thục underlined this combative stance with his choice of episcopal motto: *Miles Christi* — Soldier of Christ.

The reaction was rather predictable — some European missionaries refused to serve under Bishop Thục. The French security police regarded Thục's nomination as ominous because it was so well-received by anti-French nationalists, who saw it as a boost to their cause. It also drew increased attention to the politics of the Ngô family in general.[8] In Bishop Thục's estimation, as well as being recognition of the 'holiness and intellect' of the Vietnamese clergy, his consecration as bishop was a step forward for Viet independence and autonomy, to which his whole family were committed. The Ngô brothers regarded their upbringing as both "Confucian and Catholic,"[9] and the culture of the family was quintessentially a fusion of identities and ideals. As a priest and bishop Thục fiercely defended the idea of local interpretations of Catholicism — he was well in advance of Vatican II in this sense. In this context he promoted the increasing localization or 'Vietnamization' of the clergy and encouraged the departure of the European missionaries.[10] Outsiders could never truly understand the complexity of Asian Catholicism, in which, as the Jesuit Aloysius Pieris wrote, "Christianity does not compete with other religions but complements them[11] ... The result is neither 'syncretism ... nor 'synthesis' ... but a *symbiosis* of religions."[12] Thục would later complain about Catholicism's tendency toward "the leveling of all particularities inherent in every civilization — which, by the way, is the work of the good God, who takes pleasure in Unity and also in Diversity."[13]

"The Vatican invents regulations to quash whatever peculiarity, whether liturgical or canonical, of the 'lesser' Churches. It wants uniformity everywhere, without thinking that each people possesses its own characteristics just as respectable as those of Rome. Here are some examples: for the Roman, as a sign of respect, one stands up; in Vietnam, we kneel. The Roman extends his arms in prayer; the Vietnamese clasps his hands together to pray. Europeans shake hands as a sign of friendship or by way of greeting; Asians, Chinese, Vietnamese, put their hands together and bow their head, and the bow will be deeper according to the respectability of the one we are greeting."[14]

Diversity, Thục wrote, "is the ornament of the Universe. Why impose a single way of celebrating Holy Mass — which consists solely of the Consecration — and to impose this, under pain of suspension and even excommunication; is this not the abuse of power?"[15] This was the Viêt spirit and Viêt patriotism which Thục believed in as part of his supposed royal ancestral inheritance. He saw no contradiction with Catholicism as long as he was free to interpret it and exercise it in his own way — he was, after all, a bishop. This outlook would go a long way towards explaining his later exploits. The considerable agreement between Thục's statements of 1938 and those of 1976 (in his autobiographical notes) indicates a remarkable consistency and coherence in his vision. Whatever else may have changed in the intervening time, his understanding of being a bishop was clear, and he cherished having a free hand. Thục had also been named a papal legate, which effectively meant that he had emergency powers in case communications with the Vatican were cut off. This was an understandable precaution considering that Vietnam's neighbor, China, had already been at war with Japan since 1937, and the whole Asia-Pacific situation was unprecedentedly volatile. By the time of Thục's consecration World War Two had already effectively begun. Much would be made of Thục's emergency powers in later years, with claims that he thereby had the right in perpetuity to travel around consecrating and ordaining whomsoever he wished.[16] But it is absurd to suggest that a bishop would be granted the power to persistently overturn Church teaching, theology, and Canon Law. In fact, Thục was explicitly made a papal legate in keeping with the specific purposes and functions which were made clear to him at that time of impending war.

The newly-created vicariate of Vinh Long had about 60 priests and one million inhabitants in total — about ten percent of whom were Catholics (today there are twice as many Catholics, but the total population has increased fourfold). The *nouveau* Bishop Thục met with an ambivalent reception on arrival in Vinh Long. Some French Catholics feared that the Faith would be put in danger under a native bishop, whom they assumed was either a convert or the son of converts, and therefore not very steadfast in the

Faith. Furthermore, the vicariate was poorly resourced — Vinh Long town itself, the episcopal see, had no bishop's residence. The town's one priest, a missionary, was in France on leave when Thục arrived.[17] There was a lunch given for Thục's ceremonial taking possession of the vicariate, but he was then left alone with nobody to cook his dinner. His brothers Khôi and Diệm had come for the occasion, but since the French priest's vacant house only had one bed, the two mandarin brothers slept on benches at a parishioner's house. It was an inauspicious start. "I could hardly foresee that Vinh Long would become my solace, and that its clergy would back me wholeheartedly in organizing that no-man's-land, and that our rapport would be truly brotherly."[18]

In the meantime Thục soon acquired a young houseboy, Tri — "endowed with extraordinary laziness"[19] — and a chef, Vinh — "a very good cook but [also] a very good friend of rice alcohol, the French soldiers' 'chum-chum.'"[20] For buildings, money, and resources, as a mere off-cut from the Saigon diocese, Vinh Long got the short straw. Thục traveled around his vicariate on a bulky old French bicycle until some of his former students pooled their money to buy him a second-hand Citroën car. He was at least permitted to send the older Vinh Long seminarians to study in Saigon, since Vinh Long had no seminary either. Human resources were also a problem: to Saigon went "the best priests and to Vinh Long [went] those of less worth, and even some of doubtful virtue."[21] Thục's response to the latter seems, to put it mildly, shocking and inadequate:

"I had to write to Bishop Dumortier [of Saigon] asking him for a priest. He had the kindness, or perhaps the good fortune, to rid himself of a doubtful priest, by sending me Father 'H' who … was a sexual deviant and an utter crook. I discovered this too late. He is dead, God rest his soul. … I was obliged to send [another] young curate back to Monsignor Dumortier — young in years but vicious beyond his age. Bishop Dumortier would not take him back. Besides, shortly afterwards the poor boy ditched his cassock. Better that way. He made a living as a schoolteacher thanks to the education he had received in the minor seminary."[22]

35

Archbishop Thục's frank memoir offers us a worryingly bleak and blasé account of his mishandling or non-handling of these sexual misconduct cases. It is almost textbook willful negligence:

> "Bishop Dumortier expected me to send back more priests, but these cases, though certainly unfortunate, were not common knowledge. I was happy to admonish the guilty in secret or to send them to do a retreat. Being from Central Vietnam, where such cases were extremely rare, I was astounded to discover so many weaknesses. I spoke to Msgr. Dumortier. Here's his answer: 'It is because it is too hot in Cochin-China.' Maybe he was right. ... But the faithful, who dearly loved their priests, often turned a blind eye."[23]

There is surely little need to comment on this first-hand account. After all, were these ways of dealing with abusive priests not the norm in the Catholic Church until very recently — seek to transfer him away, send him to do a retreat, hush it up, and rely on the blind eye of the people. "Sometimes," Thục added, "I received anonymous letters. There was no need to believe them immediately."[24] And if the allegations turned out to be true?

> "I [would] reprimand him on the basis of spiritual reasons: offense to God, sacrilege for Masses said in a state of mortal sin, scandal, ineffective ministry; without showing anger, but with great compassion. Finally, I [would] ask him to suggest the spiritual punishment incurred: for example a one-week spiritual retreat, or a month in a monastery, or a change of post. I can only congratulate myself for this way of handling things."[25]

While Thục was feeling self-congratulatory in Vinh Long, his brother Diệm was still waiting for his historical moment to come. He had served in Emperor Bao Dai's government in 1933, but resigned when the French blocked their reform plans. The juvenile Bao Dai, indifferent to reforms, did not literally resign, but resigned himself to a life of debauchery instead, much to Diệm's lasting distaste.[26] Diệm's moral sensibilities may have been rooted in the Dark Ages, but politically he was still a fraction ahead of his time. He had made his name as both a Viet nationalist and an anti-communist, but politics at the end of the 1930's was not yet defined either by opposition to the French or to the Communists as it would be later. Diệm maintained his famously monastic attitude to life, which had caused Thục to observe that the Church would have been "too worldly"[27] for Diệm to make a career in it. Mysteriously, Diệm remained apart from much of the political posturing of the nineteen-thirties, clearly biding his time. Everything was to change on 22nd September 1940, when the Japanese initiated an undeclared four-day war to annex Vietnam. In the Japanese plan to control Asia and the Pacific, Vietnam did not quite have the long-term importance as other parts of Southeast Asia. It did not have the same kinds of ports or natural resources as Singapore, Malaya and Burma, but it was full of essential rice for the Japanese army and it already had a compliant local administration — the Vichy French. It was above all vital to blockade China from using Vietnam's ports, especially Haiphong. Considering the fiercely independent character of Vietnam's people, the Japanese were content to leave the French in nominal day-to-day command. Vinh Long, being in the south, came under direct French control, and Thục's movements would have been severely restricted during wartime. He therefore evacuated to Cáinhum for the duration of the war, which allowed him to travel around the diocese as before.

The onslaught of Japanese expansionism was total and overwhelming, marking the beginning of the end for the old European rulers of the region. All the nations of Southeast Asia, with the single exception of Thailand, had been under foreign colonial domination for generations, whether by the French, the British, the Dutch, or the Americans. The Japanese conquests of 1940-1942 could be seen in some lights as part of the longer-term decolonizing struggle. Hitler, during the same period, unequivocally pursued his invasion of the Baltic States, Russia, Southeast Europe, and the Caucasus purely and simply as a war of aggression, without seriously attempting to market his campaigns as liberation from Stalinist oppression. In contrast, the Japanese invaders tended to encourage the natives of the occupied states to view the Japanese as heralds of forthcoming independence. In Burma and India especially, the Japanese fostered movements purporting to work towards independence from the British. Though in reality both the Nazis and the Japanese regarded their respective conquered peoples as subhuman, many defeated Southeast Asians believed the Japanese talk of pan-Asian brotherhood and freedom. For some, in Burma for example, this pretense fed long-standing political hopes of defeating colonialism. In other cases, for example in the Japanese recruitment of Indian prisoners of war after the fall of Singapore, Japanese promises of freedom preyed on desperation and fear.

In any case, by 1942-1943 there was little reason to believe that the Japanese control of Southeast Asia would not become permanent. The situation was slightly different in Vietnam because the semblance of a French government – in Vichy – still claimed the right to continue administering France's colonies, and Vichy of course was aligned to Japan and the Axis. Even so, the Japanese were not about to leave French Indochina to its own devices, and they were the rulers and occupiers right up to the end of the war. For Ngô-dình-Diệm and others, the Japanese occupation at least presented the possibility of a future Vietnam that was neither French nor Communist. They did not necessarily see Japan and Vichy France as being on the same side — even the Axis pact was a technicality of only relative importance locally. Long-term, Japan was seen as an option for precipitating the end of French rule, allowing the possibility of a future nationalist Vietnam independent of foreign political interference. After the collapse of Vichy in 1944, Japan took full control of Vietnam, though still utilizing the local rule of the ambivalent bon vivant Bao Dai.[28] The German and Japanese losses of 1944 made an Axis victory look increasingly unlikely. The Viet nationalists' ambitions seemed to be encouraged when the Tehran Conference stated that it saw no particular advantage in restoring Indochina to French control, but after Roosevelt's death Truman and most of the international community started to shortsightedly lose interest in the Southeast

Asian mainland.[29] Within a few years however, America would be taking a very serious interest in events in Vietnam — and in the Ngô brothers, Thục and Diệm.

As World War Two drew to an end in 1945, the Ngô brothers, led by the eldest, Khôi, formed part of a broad traditionalist elite which hoped to achieve power. The nominal ruler, the Emperor Bao Dai, was not really interested in government. Khôi was a mandarin who had already served as a provincial governor. Diệm had a good reputation for opposing the French, but this was now marred by fact that he had grown tactically very close to the Japanese invaders.[30] He was always somewhat detached from reality, even in the midst of world war; above all he disliked the French way of doing politics, not primarily because of their colonialism or Vichy fascism, but because their revolutionary principles were traditionally associated with socialism and anticlericalism.[31] The Ngôs' approach seemed too high-minded for their fellow politicians, and their influence was limited to the Catholics within the elite. Diệm was still a rising star, but he was oblivious to diplomacy, tact, or public image. It was well known that he had supported the Japanese, and he even resided in quarters within the Japanese military hospital in Saigon. He did not seem to grasp what this level of collusion signified in the world of 1945. The Japanese had even come close to inviting him to form a government in the final months of the war, but at the time Diệm still objected to working under "the discredited playboy Bao Dai."[32] The Japanese for their part soon decided that Diệm and the Ngôs were too power-hungry and self-serving, fearing that they would try to create a family-run regime and raise their own secret police force.[33] It is ironic that the mistake narrowly avoided by the Japanese in 1945 was to be made by the Americans ten years later.

The opportunity for Vietnam to make a clean sweep came in August 1945 with the fall of the Japanese. Apart from all their internal squabbling, the traditional political elites were seen as either too favorable to the French or, as in the case of Bao Dai and the Ngôs, too cozy with the erstwhile Japanese occupiers.[34] There were calls for revenge against those regarded as traitors. Both Diệm and Khôi were arrested, and Khôi was shot (not buried alive as some sources state).[35] The brothers were certainly pro-Japanese, though to what extent their collaborationism was in fact simply opportunism or survivalism is difficult to discern. In fairness to them, not even the Viet-minh had led a particularly aggressive resistance movement against the Japanese occupation.[36] Ho-chi-Minh himself took a balanced view rather than a fanatically partisan one; these pro-Japanese nationalists were, Ho said, "weathercocks who were pro-French yesterday, pro-Jap today, and pro-someone else tomorrow."[37] There was at least one push by the returning non-Vichy French to prosecute Diệm for collaborationism, but only his brother Khôi paid the ultimate price.[38] The French security forces did not oppose the summary elimination of characters like Khôi — Viet nationalism was even more of a concern to them than communism, which they regarded as the lesser threat to their rule.[39] This was in part because the recent period of suppression of French authority by the Japanese had shown up the vulnerability and fallibility of French power.

The Communist Party may have visibly led the Revolution of 1945, but only at the head of a diverse popular front — this was by design, and it was Ho-chi-Minh's idea. Membership in the popular front was as much nationalist as communist, and the Communist Party itself attracted recruits for its nationalist stance rather than for pure communism. The name 'Viet-minh' in fact means 'Viet nationalist.' The Japanese were now gone and the pro-Japanese and pro-French cliques were distrusted, which left the indifferent puppet ruler Bao Dai as the only practical alternative. Against this backdrop, Ho-chi-Minh became the nearest thing to a national figurehead in both north and south.[40] It is completely erroneous to imagine at this stage a clearly delineated stand-off between communists and nationalists. "The Viet is above all a patriot, whether communist or anti-communist. [Both] Ho-chi-Minh and Ngô-dinh-Diệm are Viet through and through,"[41] Thục later observed. Thục himself was arrested by the French colonial police in October 1945, accused of encouraging youngsters to join the Communist Pioneer Youth League in Vinh Long — a charge which Thục admitted, explaining later that the Communists' aims and the united Vietnam's aims were not in his view incompatible.[42] In January 1946 Ho-chi-Minh invited Diệm to join the popular front, but received short shrift from Diệm because of the fate of his brother Khôi.[43] Ho apologized for Khôi's killing and granted safe passage to Diệm,[44] who was prepared to go on biding his time. In any case the return of the French administration cut the revolution short, but it paved the way for the bloody and lengthy Indochina war (1946-1954). It was still not yet Diệm's moment, and he would contrive to spend the key years of the ensuing war in hiding and then in exile. What he needed was a little help from his brother. Diệm went to live with Thục in Vinh Long when the Indochina war started, and with his usual flexibility of loyalties even spent some time working as a liaison officer for the French.[45] After Khôi's death in 1945, Thục had become the senior brother, and as tradition dictated, he was now the head of the family or 'second father.' However, it was also becoming clear that Nhu, the wily younger brother, would serve as the fixer, *consigliere*, and effective right-hand man to Diệm.[46]

By around 1950 Thục had begun meeting up in Saigon with Cardinal Francis Spellman of New York and had begun to request American backing for the idea of a Catholic-led Vietnam.[47] Spellman was regarded as the most politically powerful cleric of his time, and he was to become one of Diệm's most powerful advocates. Thục and Diệm hatched a plan: they applied for permission to travel to Rome for the Holy Year celebrations at the Vatican. However, they also detoured via Japan in order to enlist further support for a seizure of power by Diệm. They had meetings with Wesley Fishel, an American academic with a shadowy résumé of US government work — some sources suggest that the 'academic' was probably CIA.[48] Fishel was a proponent of the anti-colonial and anti-communist 'third force' approach to politics in Asia, and he was impressed enough with Diệm and Thục to help the brothers organize more contacts and meetings in the United

States to enlist support. The outbreak of the Korean War and the onset of McCarthyism had highlighted the imperative of fostering an anti-communist bastion in Southeast Asia.

Thục and Diệm flew to America next, where they were given a reception at the State Department with the Acting Secretary of State James Webb and William S.B. Lacy.[49] It seems that the more gregarious Thục did most of the talking and made the better impression.[50] Diệm also further strengthened ties with Cardinal Spellman, often meeting with him and then-Senator Kennedy. With Spellman's help Diệm began to garner huge support within right-wing and Catholic circles.[51] American interests were anti-communist interests, and the Ngôs were seen to offer the right kind of stability to keep Ho-chi-Minh in check. Acting Secretary of State James Webb saw clearly that Thục's influence on the future regime was not to be underestimated.[52] The CIA duly made a point of establishing meaningful contact with Thục, regarding him as part of the future triumvirate along with Nhu and Diệm.[53] The goal became to get the Ngôs into power — it was not regarded as particularly important that they be democratically mandated: "The United States wanted an anticommunist government in Saigon — democratic or not."[54]

During this same period, younger brother Nhu had begun organizing what would become the Can Lao Party — the Personalist Labor Revolutionary Party — with brother number four Cân's help. The Can Lao Party would be a form of nationalism that the Ngô family could shape and control, to provide a formal framework for their ambitions. Nhu also worked to infiltrate the labor unions in Saigon.[55] From 1951 onwards he also became the Ngô family's regular day-to-day contact with the CIA working in Vietnam.[56] Nhu was married by now. In 1943 he had wed Trần-lệ-Xuân, fifteen years his junior, who would become known simply as Madame Nhu. She had converted to Catholicism in order to marry Nhu, and would not only support her husband unquestioningly but also share unelected power with him. Madame Nhu was also devoted to her brother-in-law Diệm, and was effectively the only woman to feature in his life apart from his mother and sisters, becoming de facto First Lady. Attractive, confident, and photogenic, Madame Nhu would probably have welcomed comparisons to Eva Perón, though the similarities to Elena Ceauşescu are more striking. Madame Nhu was manipulative, insensitive, power-hungry, and fiercely loyal to her family, whose delusions she shared in and stoked. She joins Grace Mugabe, Imelda Marcos, and Lady Macbeth in the female powerbroker hall of infamy. After Thục, Diệm, and Nhu (and Madame Nhu), brother number four was the quieter Cân, remaining up in Huế, who managed to stay out of the limelight the longest and was still unknown in the early nineteen-fifties.[57] Cân, in Thục's opinion, worked the hardest to build the Can Lao Party: "It was Cân who organized the powerful political party that sustained the politics of my brothers Diệm and Nhu. He managed to secure the considerable funds that are necessary for any political organization, through the cinnamon trade"[58] — and also, as Thục probably knew, through opium trafficking.[59]

January 1951 found Diệm still in America, where he had decided to stay. He spent the next two and a half years as a guest of the Maryknoll Fathers — the Catholic Foreign Missions Society of America — and resided at their Seminary in Lakewood, New Jersey. He was thus close enough to Washington to go buttonholing State Department officials and Congressmen, persuading them to cold-shoulder the French.[60] Diệm's moment came almost by default. In June 1953 he left the United States for Europe again, and after a brief stay at a monastery in Belgium, his brother Thục managed to arrange an audience with Pope Pius XII. With Thục's support, Diệm's credibility and influence were rising to all-time highs. June 1953 was also the month that Nguyễn-van-Thuận, Thục's nephew, was ordained priest. Like his uncle before him, Thuận was then sent to do further studies in Rome.

Emboldened by his rising stock, Diệm took up the nationalist cause once more. Meanwhile, in the war that Diệm had avoided, the massive and decisive battle of Dien Bien Phu in May 1954 constituted a catastrophic and conclusive defeat of the French. Dien

Bien Phu sent shockwaves across the world, appearing to mark the turning of the tide against the colonial powers in Southeast Asia; the Dutch had already conceded complete independence to Indonesia, and within a year the British would seek talks leading to the independence of Malaya and Singapore. Within Vietnam, the display of force and tenacity by the tiny Viet-minh drastically raised the stakes and reinforced the American imperative to stop the spread of communism in the region. In June 1954, while the Geneva Conference to formally end the Indochina war was still in progress, Bao Dai, as Head of State, asked Diệm to become Prime Minister of South Vietnam. In a ceremony at Cannes, Diệm swore on the Bible not to betray Bao Dai — an oath the supposedly devout Diệm would break soon afterwards.[61] After eight years, the Indochina War finally ended, and Diệm was heading home as Prime Minister. The Ngós were in power now, and Thục's diocesan HQ became a training base for Nhu's brand new secret police force.[62]

Notes

[1]   Ngô-dinh-Thục, talking about the establishment of Catholicism in Vietnam; in hindsight his words also seem prophetic. Quoted in Charles Keith, *Catholic Vietnam: a Church from Empire to Nation,* University of California Press, Berkeley CA, 2012, p 177

[2]   Ngô-dinh-Thục, 'Misericordias Domini in Aeternum Cantabo: Autobiographie de Mgr. Pierre Martin Ngô-Dinh-Thục, Archeveque de Huế' [sic], *Einsicht* (Special Edition), Una Voce-Gruppe Maria, Munich, August 1982, p 29

[3]   Cf. Ngô-dinh-Thục, op. cit. p 28

[4]   Ngô-dinh-Thục, op. cit. p 28

[5]   Quoted in Charles Keith, *Catholic Vietnam: a Church from Empire to Nation,* 2012, p 177

[6]   Ibid.

[7]   Ibid.

[8]   Cf. Charles Keith, op. cit. p 177

[9]   James S. Olson and Randy Roberts, *Where the Domino Fell: America and Vietnam 1945 to 1990,* St. Martin's Press, New York, 1991, p 55

[10]   Cf. Charles Keith, op. cit. p 177

[11] Aloysius Pieris, 'Political Theologies in Asia,' Ch. 18 in Peter Scott and William T. Cavanaugh (Eds), *The Blackwell Companion to Political Theology,* Blackwell, Oxford, 2004, [pp 256-270], pp 261-262

[12] Aloysius Pieris, op. cit. p 263

[13] Ngô-dinh-Thục, op. cit. p 9

[14] Idem p 10

[15] Idem pp 9-10

[16] Cf. Guérard des Lauriers, interview, *Sodalitium* (Spanish edition) No. 13, March 1988, p 10

[17] Cf. Ngô-dinh-Thục, op. cit. pp 28-29

[18] Ngô-dinh-Thục, op. cit. p 29

[19] Idem p 30

[20] Idem p 29

[21] Idem p 30

[22] Idem p 32

[23] Ibid.

[24] Ngô-dinh-Thục, op. cit. p 33

[25] Ibid.

[26] Cf. *New York Times,* 14th May 1972, p 16

[27] David Halberstam, *The Making of a Quagmire,* Random House, New York, 1965, p 41

[28] Stein Tønnesson, *The Vietnamese Revolution of 1945: Roosevelt, Ho Chi Minh and De Gaulle in a World at War,* (PRIO Monographs, Oslo), Sage Publications, London, 1991, p 96

[29] Cf. David Halberstam, op. cit. p 34

[30] Cf. Stein Tønnesson, op. cit. p 105

[31] Cf. Idem p 96

[32] David Halberstam, op. cit. p 36

[33] Cf. Stein Tønnesson, op. cit. p 284

[34] Cf. Hilaire du Berrier, *Background to Betrayal: The Tragedy of Vietnam,* Western Islands, Belmont MA, 1965, p 13

[35] Cf. Stein Tønnesson, op. cit. p 96

[36] Cf. Hilaire du Berrier, op. cit. p 7

[37] Quoted in Stein Tønnesson, op. cit. p 105

[38] Cf. Hilaire du Berrier, op. cit. p 162

[39] Cf. Stein Tønnesson, op. cit. p 105

[40] Cf. David Halberstam, op. cit. p 37

[41] Ngô-dinh-Thục, op. cit. p 9

[42] Cf. Spencer C. Tucker (ed), *The Encyclopedia of the Vietnam War, a Political, Social, and Military History,* ABC-CLIO, Santa Barbara CA, 2011, p 813

[43] Cf. David Halberstam, op. cit. p 40

[44] Cf. *New York Times,* 14th May 1972, p 16
[45] Ibid.
[46] Cf. A.J. Langguth, *Our Vietnam: The War 1954-1975,* Simon & Schuster, New York, 2000, p 90
[47] Cf. Spencer C. Tucker, op. cit. p 813
[48] Cf. Hilaire du Berrier, op. cit. p 99
[49] Cf. Spencer C. Tucker, op. cit. p 813
[50] Cf. Seth Jacobs, *America's Miracle Man in Vietnam: Ngo Dinh Diệm, Religion, Race, and U.S. Intervention in Southeast Asia,* Duke University Press, Durham NC, 2004, p 26
[51] Cf. James S. Olson and Randy Roberts, op. cit. p 64
[52] Cf. Seth Jacobs, op. cit. pp 26-27
[53] Cf. Thomas L. Ahern Jr., *CIA and the House of Ngô: covert action in South Vietnam, 1954-1963 (Unclassified),* Center for the Study of Intelligence, Washington, 2000, p 14 and p 22
[54] James S. Olson and Randy Roberts, op. cit. p 64
[55] Cf. Hilaire du Berrier, op. cit. p 28
[56] Cf. Thomas L. Ahern Jr., op. cit. p 22
[57] Cf. Hilaire du Berrier, op. cit. p 28
[58] Ngô-dinh-Thục, op. cit. p 23
[59] Cf. James S. Olson and Randy Roberts, op. cit. p 99
[60] Cf. Hilaire du Berrier, op. cit. p 24
[61] Cf. *New York Times,* 14th May 1972, p 16
[62] Cf. Spencer C. Tucker, op. cit. p 813

III

CAPITULUM TERTIUM

'HE CELEBRATES THE NATIONAL CULT'[1] — THE MAKING OF A CATASTROPHE

All French influence and control over Vietnam was eradicated. France's power had declined in counterpoint to the rise of Diệm's support in America and Europe, which Thục had been instrumental in facilitating and nurturing. Before long, "South Vietnam was an independent nation wallowing in American money."[2] Elections were scheduled, but the Diệm camp would feel no particular obligation to see that they were fair or transparent; the United States, too, was more interested in the result being anti-communist than honest. Though technically only appointed as Bao Dai's Prime Minister, Diệm immediately began implementing his vision of absolute rule; 'interviews' with the new Premier — effectively barrages of spiel — could last from 3 to 10 *hours*. The onset of paranoia, characteristic of an autocrat, was also immediate; he feared conspiracy, revolution and assassination, apparently "with good reason,"[3] many felt. But Diệm's take on premiership was no secret; he had outlined his intended approach, stressing the required moral virtues and obligations, in an article written before he assumed power. He entitled it, with apparently unintended irony, 'Democratic Development in Vietnam.' Diệm referred to the 'basic principle' of maintaining 'the mystique of government,' explaining that the ideal state official 'must conduct himself as one participating in a religious rite.' The 'sovereign,' in Diệm's quasi-sacramental conception of leadership, is due 'sacred respect' as 'the mediator between the people and heaven as he celebrates the national cult.' It was in the framework of this philosophy that Diệm, increasingly with Nhu's help, crafted and projected his own peculiar personality cult in South Vietnam.[4]

Bao Dai had arguably been left with no option other than to invite Diệm to become his Prime Minister. No other active politician at that time had the same credentials, resources, organization, and — thanks to Thục — powerful connections and support from overseas. Bao Dai was also pretty sure that Diệm's connections would bring in large consignments of foreign money. But Diệm turned his back on the Geneva agreements, including the commitment to hold a vote on reunification, and in October 1955 he deposed Bao Dai. After a fraudulent referendum organized by Nhu, Diệm declared himself President of what he proclaimed the Republic of Vietnam (South Vietnam). Thục thus became part of the ruling family, presiding jointly over a dictatorship in which the power was unequivocally concentrated in the hands of the Ngôs, enforced through secret police, heavy censorship, and the imprisonment and torture of opponents. Diệm cultivated his image as the "miracle man"[5] of Vietnam, the man of the hour who appeared to achieve the impossible. He resettled nearly a million refugees fleeing from the newly-established North Vietnam — mostly Catholics, "herded in a mass exodus by their priests."[6] It was hard to believe that Diệm had begun his mandarinate career three decades earlier, touring rural districts on horseback in a brocaded robe and lampshade hat;[7] now he was the very modern "Mandarin in a sharkskin suit,"[8] crushing gambling, prostitution, and narcotics gangs in Saigon that had previously operated under French police protection. The opium seized from the Saigon gangs was moved north to be trafficked in and out of the country by Ngô-dinh-Can.[9]

Early successes made the Ngô family think that they could do no wrong. Diệm's timing was good; his triumphant arrival on the scene was synonymous with the end of the war and the end of colonialism. He came like a prophet from afar, who had stood up to the French and now eliminated the residual colonial corruption that the Viet people were sick of. But the pressures upon this national savior were overwhelming for his ethereal personality — fatally, his solution was to retreat into the support of his "large and forceful family."[10] They too believed in their infallibility and untouchability, and in maintaining that unapproachable 'mystique' of leadership;[11] the Ngôs believed in Diệm, and they believed in each other. Diệm soon began to see his brother Nhu and sister-in-law Madame Nhu as the pillars of his regime, with Thục in third place. It was completely *cosa nostra*, a concentrated family affair. As Madame Nhu explained, tactlessly and "to all who would listen, ...'Without his family he [Diệm] stands alone. The women follow me and my husband has his Youth Movement. The Catholics take orders from Archbishop Thục.'"[12] Thục's role was much more than just dealing with religious matters, however, and his importance to the regime should not be underestimated. The CIA considered it essential to meet with him and maintain contact with him, in addition to Diệm and Nhu.[13] They too saw Thục as being number three in the family hierarchy, after Diệm and the Nhus. But it was Thục who boasted of the most efficient "circle of political contacts"[14] in the CIA's estimations.

Having taken power, Diệm quickly began consolidating it by sharing it out among the family. Throughout his leadership he would feel the need to underline the Catholic affiliation of the regime, and also to demonstrate that his power worked both ways — that as a Catholic head of state Diệm could put pressure on the Church as well. What better way to achieve these ends than by arranging a 'red hat' for Thục; if Diệm could secure the rank of Cardinal for his brother, it would also be a fitting thank-you for assisting him on the road to the Presidency. The first step would be for Diệm, never famed for his diplomacy and tact, to strongly suggest that Thục be appointed Archbishop of Saigon, but the Vatican, unimpressed with recent events in Vietnam, would not play ball. The response from Rome was documented by *France-Soir* of 26th October 1955, just two days after the rigged referendum:

"The only shadow on the scene for Mr. Diệm is paradoxically the attitude of the Vatican. The Vatican has just named as Bishop of Saigon, not the candidate of Mr. Diệm, who is his own brother, Monsignor Thục, but an unknown priest named Hien. The blow for the President of the Council [Diệm] is harder, since Mr. Hien is considered lukewarm where he is concerned."[15]

Diệm was livid, while Thục pragmatically boarded the next plane to Rome, in order to protest to the Curia in person. *France-Soir* of 29th December 1955 revealed that as the Ngôs waited for the outcome of Thục's direct appeal to the Vatican to have Hien's appointment overturned, the papal order naming Hien as apostolic vicar of Saigon was intercepted and detained by Diệm's postal authorities, with its seals broken and the contents photocopied. "The Vatican maintained its decision,"[16] wrote *France-Soir,* "and Vietnamese censors suppressed the announcement of Hien's elevation for several weeks, until priests decided to announce the news from their pulpits and Hien himself used the word excommunication in regard to Diệm."[17]

These blatant attempts to manipulate Church affairs did not go unnoticed. In a radio show on 29th November and a press release of 5th December, the National Catholic Welfare Conference representative, Father Patrick O'Connor, lambasted Diệm's shameless interference in trying to finagle the Saigon job for Thục. The Irish Fr. O'Connor's attack hit Diệm and the Ngôs where it hurt — among their influential Catholic supporters in the US. *America,* the Jesuit magazine, editorialized Fr. O'Connor's reports in its 10th December 1955 issue, observing that

"News that the government of South Vietnam is resorting to press censorship is disturbing enough. That the censorship should be coupled with interference in Church administration is downright perplexing, particularly since the free world has been given to understand that Pres. Ngô-dinh-Diệm and democratic government are practically synonymous terms. According to [a National Catholic Welfare Conference] report dated November 26, the Vietnamese government has been indulging in some pretty childish antics in

50

Saigon. … Censoring all news of Msgr. Hien's impending consecration, the Government has requested the Holy See to change
the appointment. While the authorities are not expected to interfere with the consecration, the whispering campaign against the
Bishop-elect and the ill will it has caused may continue to foment
trouble. Moreover, Fr. O'Connor sees in the incident a reflection
of a growing tendency in Vietnam to interfere in Church affairs.
Priests' letters are opened in the post office. Rumors abound that
the Church, bishops, priests and Catholic organizations may be in
for government regimentation. The outcome may even be indirect
restrictions on preaching and pressure on foreign missionaries to
get out of Vietnam. This review has constantly supported Ngô-
dinh-Diệm, not on the ground of his Catholicism, but because he
seemed to be the only available political figure capable of unifying
Vietnam's variety of political-religious factions and ushering in an
era of truly representative government. We trust our confidence is
not about to be destroyed."[18]

After just one year of Western-oriented and supposedly Catholic
government, the Catholic Church in Vietnam was bracing itself for
state-imposed restrictions and interference comparable to China.
But the Vatican proved capable of asserting itself: interestingly,
Thục was not just rebuffed in attempting to sway the Hien case
in his favor, but he was actually required to consecrate Monsignor
Hien to the episcopate personally. The Vatican also instructed
him to consecrate, at the same time, Monsignor Binh, with whom
Thục also had serious and open conflicts, especially later when
it would be Binh who succeeded Hien as Archbishop of Saigon
in 1960. These facts help to dismantle the notion that Thục, as
papal legate, selected and consecrated bishops freely.[19] The French
Dominican Guérard des Lauriers stated decades later that Thục
had told him about this; Thục claimed to have personally selected
and consecrated all the Vietnamese bishops throughout the 1940's
(in fact he did no consecrations in the 1940's) and 1950's (he did
only two consecrations in the 1950's — his archrivals Hien and
Binh).[20] The suggestion that Hien and Binh, of all people, were
Thục's personal free choices is not credible. In any case, these

consecrations were properly mandated from Rome, not from Thục. He was certainly never mandated to play fast and loose with Canon Law. The Vatican affirmed its control in Vietnam and kept Thục on a short leash — trusted (as legate) to do the two consecrations at Rome's bidding, whether he liked their choice or not.

Disappointments did not sit well with Thục, and the resentment was building up. But just as Thục had developed his own self-absolving ways to deal with sex-abusing priests, he unapologetically produced a strategy for consolidating his own personal powerbases; making full use of the free hand he enjoyed as a key member of the regime, Thục began amassing vast amounts of wealth, power, and real estate for himself and the Church. Hilaire du Berrier wrote that:

> "[Thục] plunged into business with gusto, buying apartment houses, stores, rubber estates and timber concessions. When Thục set his eyes on a piece of real estate, other bidders prudently dropped out. Importation of schoolbooks was in his hands, which gave him the rights of a censor, and Michigan State University a market. Soldiers, instead of building defenses, were put to work cutting wood for brother Thục to sell. Army trucks and labor were requisitioned to build buildings for him."[21]

Thục was not averse to even more direct methods for raising hard cash either: a businessman commented that "his requests for donations read like tax notices."[22] It should be noted that Hilaire du Berrier, though clearly one of Thục and the Ngôs' bluntest critics, was not politically biased — he was himself a vehement and vociferous anti-communist. Other equally fierce critics of the regime, however, found Thục likeable at a personal level. Thục's activities still did not go unnoticed at the Vatican — his behavior in these years goes a long way towards explaining the cold shoulder he would receive in Rome later on. The Vatican was also concerned about the Ngôs' urging of Catholics in the north to uproot and flee as refugees to the south. Thục and Diệm saw this displacement as desirable because the refugees were likely to become loyal supporters of the Ngô regime.[23]

By now the south was the domain of the default First Lady, Nhu's "tyrannical wife"[24] Madame Nhu. Her pet project was her 'Women's Solidarity Movement.'[25] Innocuous as it may sound, its members drew military officers' pay and were armed with brand-new American carbines, while front-line troops used Remington rifles dated 1917.[26] Madame Nhu relished the external trappings of leadership, the ceremonies and award-giving. Behind the celebrity smile there was a famously acid tongue. Though Madame Nhu was the Catholic convert of the family, her sharp comments "spared no-one, not even the Pope."[27] In terms of her practical contributions to the regime, the First Lady banned divorce,[28] dancing,[29] and large portions of press activity. It did not take long for someone to label her "the Vietnamese Lady MacBeth".[30] She expelled any journalists who she felt painted her in a bad light, such as when she was reported — accurately — as saying that "the [Communist] enemy has more drive."[31] Hostility towards the press was not exclusive to Madame Nhu, however; the whole Ngô regime sought to keep the press under its thumb and hurled abuse at journalists when they did not toe the line.[32]

Since the Ngôs considered themselves infallible, they never sought outside advice, whether on civil planning, social issues, or military strategy. They convened no experts, advisers, or consultants from outside of the family. As a result they squandered resources and constantly changed their minds on major projects. Though neither Diệm, nor Nhu, nor anyone else in the family had ever served in the armed forces, they considered themselves top military tacticians.[33] "Diệm's right to rule by decree in any emergency was tantamount to the 'divine right' he believed he deserved in his own conception of holding the heavenly mandate,"[34] the *New York Times* recalled. Diệm became renowned for his many-hour-long sermons, haranguing friends and foes alike — he was a monologist rather than a conversationalist. Big national celebrations and parades created a paradox — Diệm feared assassination so he filled Saigon with soldiers, but in fact the greatest potential danger to him was a military coup from within the army itself. He therefore made the

Presidential Guard predominantly Catholic and armed them to the teeth, leaving the regular army fighting the guerrilla war in the north starved of troops and vehicles.[35] Diệm's understanding of his inherent right to rule stemmed partly from his confidence in his personal moral righteousness, but this was infused with paranoia and suspicion of everyone and everything outside of the family. The Ngôs had a private conception of the meaning of Catholicism, and this family religion made the austere Diệm what he was: "He, who could never have been corrupted by worldly goods, became corrupted by power and pride."[36]

Thục was the same: he had great confidence in his own abilities and standing, and he had no hesitation in flying to Rome and trying to knock the Vatican into line when he saw fit. In later years it became clear that in Thục's estimations, by way of his status as a papal legate, he ruled by a kind of divine right as well, like his brother Diệm. Thục idolized Diệm and they were equals, but there was a special place in his heart for the unsung hero, his brother Cân:

> "It was Cân who organized the powerful political party that sustained the politics of my brothers Diệm and Nhu. He managed to secure the considerable funds necessary for any political organization, through the cinnamon trade [and opium trafficking].[37] Cân, with no political mandate, and without being able to speak French, managed to become the unofficial governor of Central Vietnam. He ... owned ships and managed millions of Piasters. He was a force to be reckoned with."[38]

Thục's pride in all of his brothers' achievements shines through his words, uncritically and unapologetically; they were beyond reproach. If money, weapons, rice, schoolbooks, real estate, and opium existed as part of God's great plan, then they were there for the Ngôs to manipulate and use as they wished. Thục had upgraded his personal transportation by this time, from the old Citroën, bought by former students, to a fleet of cars consisting of a Mercedes, a Versailles, and a Jeep. "The latter two cars were gifts from benefactors; the Mercedes I bought myself, thanks to saving up the hard currency allotted to me by the government for my overseas trips."[39] Like Diệm, Thục never really accepted that he could not always do whatever he wanted. "Monsignor Thục wished to hold an anticommunist meeting in Saigon [but] Monsignor Bình, the [new] archbishop of the capital, refused, saying, 'I am the master of the diocese of Saigon and I am not going to let my cathedral become a headquarters for political meetings."[40] It was not that Archbishop Bình of Saigon was soft on communism — the absolute opposite was true — "it was simply that in his eyes Monsignor Thục was not fighting communism but using the Communist threat to politick for his family."[41]

But even reporters who were critical of the Ngôs still saw Thục's good qualities, it must be said. He was seen as "a relaxed man blessed with congeniality and a fine sense of humor."[42] He managed to balance his twin roles as a member of the ruling junta and a member of the clergy, displaying "great political skills as well as a genuinely spiritual nature."[43] As a bishop he was perhaps unruly, but he was not disobedient when push came to shove — he did not just go around consecrating the bishops he wanted to consecrate, as he later claimed, and he did consecrate those he was instructed to consecrate, no more. In 1957 the bishops of Vietnam were exhorted by Pope Pius XII to found a new Catholic university. Thục took up the challenge and succeeded against considerable odds in founding the University of Dalat, with his "bare hands and an empty wallet … a miracle of God's goodness, bestowed upon the descendants of three centuries of martyrs."[44] He became the university's first Chancellor, and as the decade neared its end his reputation and standing began to improve considerably. These years saw new winds begin to blow through the worldwide Catholic Church — it was now the era of Pope John XXIII.

24th November 1960 brought a number of changes in the Vietnamese Catholic Church: Vinh Long became a Diocese, and Saigon and Huế became Archdioceses. With his prior sins forgiven and good work rewarded, Thục was nominated Archbishop of Huế by John XXIII. Thục was at that time living in the Presidential

Palace along with Nhu, Madame Nhu, and Diệm. But it was a time of mixed fortunes. November 1960 also saw the first serious attempt at a coup to oust the Ngôs, and a year later there was the bombing of the Presidential Palace by two distinguished air-force pilots.[45] The Ngôs survived the bombing with a few scratches, but the sumptuous palace was damaged beyond the possibility of safe restoration. The Ngôs immediately ploughed a fortune in US Dollars into building the new 120,000 square meter Presidential Palace, which survives today in Ho-Chi-Minh City — renamed the Independence Palace or Reunification Palace. Relocated safely back up in Huế, Thục continued to acquire farms, businesses, urban real estate, rental property and rubber plantations.[46] He built a new seminary, not with the proceeds of his businesses however, but with 'donations' — "of which only God knows the figures"[47] — given "generously and discreetly"[48] by Diệm from government funds.

Cân continued to complain about Thục abusing his powers, using 'his' troops to chop wood and work on church buildings, and 'his' army vehicles to transport materials.[49] This was a little rich coming from Cân, considering that he himself had usurped power to become the unelected de facto ruler. But Thục was making use of a lot of privileges. The 370,000 acres (1500 square kilometers) of Catholic Church land in the country were exempt from land reform, while by law all holdings larger than 1.15 km² were liable for compulsory division and distribution. Catholics were also de facto exempt from the *corvée* (conscripted) labor service that the government obliged all citizens to perform. Although the Catholic Church could rightly complain of State interference and manipulation at high levels, Catholics overall enjoyed various kinds of immunity under the Ngô regime and the Church mostly did as it pleased. American observers were dismayed to see, sold on the market stalls of Huế, "such foodstuffs as oil, corn and cheese marked 'NOT TO BE SOLD OR EXCHANGED ... A GIFT OF THE AMERICAN PEOPLE.' Such foods, turned over to Catholic organizations to be distributed gratis through the country, were sold to swell the cash reserves of the organizations."[50] The Ngô regime displayed banners reading 'Long Live the Catholic Church' in French, Latin, and Vietnamese, and gave state receptions to visiting Catholic dignitaries such as Cardinal Spellman. During one of his visits, Spellman announced that he would donate 50,000 US Dollars to South Vietnam, explicitly saying that the aid was to be distributed among Catholics only. US aid was already widely believed to be disproportionately distributed to Catholic majority villages.

Meanwhile there were no such privileges for Buddhist organizations and they were legally considered 'private' activities with no automatic right to hold public events. This restrictive private legal status had been imposed by the French, who were well aware of the historic bond between religion and political activism in Southeast Asian culture. Official permission was therefore required in order to conduct Buddhist activities in public — all a hangover from the old colonial laws which the Ngô regime had no intention of repealing. In majority Buddhist Vietnam, the Ngôs' attitudes and policies inflamed religious tensions. The regime's bias towards Catholics in civil and military promotions was obvious, as well as land registrations, business regulations, and tax concessions. ARVN officers often converted to Catholicism in order to improve their career prospects. The issuing of firearms to village self-defense militias in the northern areas favored Catholics. Some Buddhist villages were said to have converted en masse in order to receive aid, or to avoid being forcibly resettled by the regime. Those who had converted during the regime under a sense of obligation, duress, or for career purposes, became known as "1955 Catholics."[51]

By 1961 the USA had "committed itself fully to Vietnam, and placed its prestige in Southeast Asia at stake — and in the hands of the Ngô family."[52] But America had invested its money and hopes in a rapidly failing police state.[53] David Halberstam, committing the cardinal sin of understatement, called it "a clumsy and heavy-handed government, whose population had a latent sense of discontent."[54] All of the Ngô brothers had caught the public's attention by the early sixties. Cân was making a fortune, now smuggling not only opium but also rice, Southeast Asia's number one commodity, strictly regulated and controlled, with good reason. The youngest Ngô brother, Luyen, conveniently based overseas, was becoming a multi-millionaire speculating on currency, thanks to insider information provided by his brothers.[55] Nhu, now heavily addicted to opium himself, did his best to focus on commanding his and Madame Nhu's private police forces, which they painstakingly taught to goosestep.[56] *Paris Match* magazine of 23rd November 1963 summed up the regime thus:

> "To Diệm went the power, to Nhu the police, to his wife the corruption and the deals, to Luyen diplomacy and to Cân the traffic in rice. Religion was the domain of Thục, the archbishop, with his vast landholdings and personal residence surrounded by a tower of anti-aircraft batteries."[57]

Thục appeared blissfully ignorant of impending collapse and the chaotic state of his family. The corruption, the rackets, and the drugs were common knowledge — to everyone apart from Thục, or so it seemed. Years later, still oblivious to reality, he wrote that "everyone knows and respects the names Ngô-dinh-Diệm, father of the Republic of Vietnam, and Ngô-dinh-Nhu and Ngô-dinh-Cân, aides of the President".[58] With Thục the delusions and self-deceptions of the Ngôs would outlive the regime itself. Thục's main, incredible delusion, *Paris Match* reported, was that he should now be aiming for the highest office in the Church: "the cardinal's hat was not the extent of Thục's ambition. Monsignor Thục intended to become Pope. Nothing less."[59] Diệm was right behind him. It is of course customary that the Supreme Pontiff comes from a majority Catholic country, and to this end Diệm published 'official' statistics showing that Vietnam was 70% Catholic, 20% Buddhist, and 10% other faiths.

> "The claim might have continued had an apostolic delegate not arrived on the scene in the midst of a Buddhist celebration and

had said delegate not observed that, in his opinion, considering the Buddhist oriflammes along his route, the 70% figure should apply to the faithful of the pagodas. Diệm was furious. The flying of Buddhist banners was forbidden and the immutable mechanism of repression that led to monks burning themselves in public was in motion."[60]

It was clear that Thục's career ambitions were going to be thwarted yet again. While Thục was fairly accustomed to setbacks, Diệm was deeply tormented by such blows to the family's prestige; he was gradually losing his grip. In the winter of 1962, the Ngôs' mother died. Having outlived her eldest son, the executed Khôi, who would have been 71 in 1962, she was at least spared witnessing the horrors yet to come. The regime's increasingly hostile attitude toward the Buddhist majority was reciprocated in a long history of "smoldering resentment"[61] towards the Catholics. Buddhists "resented the fact that they were second-class citizens in a country where their religion had once flowered and dominated."[62] Diệm continued to make increasingly stupid claims: Vietnam was supposedly now only 15% Buddhist, with Catholic numbers still rocketing.[63] Diệm aimed to crush the Buddhists, and only needed an opportunity.[64]

On 4th May, Archbishop Ngô-dinh-Thục celebrated twenty-five years since his episcopal consecration in 1938. Diệm, attending the celebrations in Huế, rebuked Thục for allowing (or encouraging) yellow and white papal flags to be flown everywhere.[65] This was technically in violation of a rarely-enforced law which prohibited the display of any flag other than the national one, but Diệm was probably more concerned about setting a dangerous precedent. Four days later, on 8th May 1963, the same obscure law was aggressively enforced; the Buddhists of Huế were prohibited from flying Buddhist flags on Vesak, the holiday marking the birthday of Gautama Buddha. The Buddhists' protestations led to the Army firing into the crowd, killing eight people and wounding dozens more.[66] They had fired no warning shots and made no attempt to disperse the crowd. Ludicrously, the Ngôs' initial reaction was to blame the Viet-cong, but neither the country nor the foreign press would swallow it.[67] The fuse was ignited and Vietnam exploded. Protests broke out across the country, and the regime attacked and vandalized Buddhist pagodas in response. It is estimated that hundreds died. The Kennedy administration begged Diệm to take calming and stabilizing action, but the Ngôs proved incapable of compromise or sensitivity.[68] The events highlighted the utter detachment of the regime; the simple conciliatory gestures that would come instinctively to other politicians were completely alien to the Ngôs.[69]

Of all the brothers, only the famously practical and level-headed Cân was inclined towards a strategy of reconciliation.[70] Diệm illogically dismissed the entire crisis as Communist propaganda,[71] and Thục was in total agreement with him. Buddhist organizations, Thục said, "serve as a refuge for our friends the Communists, protected from the police by the right of asylum given to the pagodas ... [and the] presence of Communists among the bonzes [Buddhist monks] is very probable since they have infiltrated even the Legion of Mary."[72] Many Catholics foresaw a rise in anti-Catholic feeling as part of the long-term effects of the crisis. Graham Greene wrote that "Diệm may well leave his tolerant country a legacy of anti-Catholicism."[73] A French priest, Father Jean Renou, with thirty-seven years of missionary experience in Asia, stated that Diệm was "undoing all we have accomplished in a hundred and fifty years! There was no ill-will between Catholics and Buddhists when he came into power. Now unless we can get him out quickly, we Catholics will suffer when he is gone."[74] Buddhism, not surprisingly, became a focus of opposition to the regime and started to attract converts, this time for more authentic reasons than Catholicism had provided. Buddhism was appreciated for being truly Vietnamese, for not being associated with the Ngôs, and simply for not being Catholicism, the source of the tyranny.[75]

One month after the start of the crisis, on 11th June, Thích-quảng-Đức, a 73-year-old Buddhist monk, set himself on fire at a busy intersection in Saigon, as a protest against the Ngô regime's ongoing oppression and persecution of Buddhists.[76] Kennedy called the photo of Thích-quảng-Đức's death the most emotional picture in history. The photographer won a Pulitzer for it. Other protest-suicides followed. Diệm was still in denial, claiming that the burning monk incident was staged by American TV, even though no TV cameras were present.[77] Diệm's "tyrannical"[78] pseudo-First Lady did nothing to inject much-needed reason or sensitivity into the crisis; Madame Nhu, "who toward the end of the regime had as much influence on Diệm as anyone,"[79] stated that she was "willing to provide the gasoline for the next barbecue."[80] Nhu himself was increasingly high on drugs, living in a megalomaniac world of his own. He was even considering making a private deal with Communist leaders in Hanoi to see his brother overthrown but his own survival assured.[81] Diệm remained in a state of utter inertia, largely brought on by the shock of realizing that his regime was not infallible. Neither domestic nor foreign pressure could coax him into making urgently needed decisions to avert further catastrophe. It was in the third week of August 1963 that Nhu, in a drug-induced paranoid fit, ordered a violent crackdown on the Buddhists; even then Diệm could not be persuaded to reign his brother in. When Diệm finally agreed to hold talks with Buddhist leaders, it was Nhu who forced him to change his mind, pushing ahead with the repression that drove more Buddhists to publicly burn themselves to death.[82]

In September 1963, at the height of the chaos, Thục prepared to depart for Rome. While he continued to live safely in his heavily-defended compound, "the entire fabric of Vietnam began to come apart."[83] The Ngôs, incredibly, responded by turning against their two main sources of support — the army and the US.[84] The religious unrest and increasingly shambolic leadership coincided with major Communist victories in the north, thus completely alienating the generals. From Washington, President Kennedy called for urgent reforms — too little too late under the circumstances, as what was really wanted was the ousting of the Ngôs. But they were going nowhere of their own accord.[85] The US, snubbed, finally began to distance itself from the Ngôs.[86] It was the start of the final act of the drama. How had it come to this? What had Diệm led the Ngô family into? Or was it they who had led Diệm? The Ngôs constituted an unusual regime, formed long ago in the bosom of the family. Thục's recollections describe the regime's earliest incarnation, in a seemingly more innocent age:

> "[Diệm] amused himself by coercing my two little sisters and my two little brothers into 'playing war.' First, he drew moustaches above their lips with a piece of charred cork, and the rifles were made from the central stalks of large banana leaves. It was comical. But for Diệm it was quite serious, and he led this army consisting of two little soldiers and two little soldierettes, and they trudged on the ground with their bare feet: *Un-deux, Un-deux*. Woe betide the distracted soldier: a sabre blow on the derriere called him or her back into line."[87]

Comical for Thục, serious for Diệm. Thục would always be blessed with the ability to take things more lightly than his brother, who had earnestly trained his little army and kept them in line — but in adulthood as in childhood, it was all a charade, and the moustaches were just painted on. The Ngôs had set the scene for the war game, but they were about to be permanently removed from play, leaving countless others to face and fight the actual war.

Notes

1   Ngô-dinh-Diệm describing the spiritual virtues of the ideal leader, as he saw it: quoted in the *New York Times*, 14th May 1972, p 16
2   Cf. James S. Olson and Randy Roberts, *Where the Domino Fell: America and Vietnam 1945 to 1990*, St. Martin's Press, New York, 1991, p 64
3   James S. Olson and Randy Roberts, op. cit. p 64
4   Cf. *New York Times*, 14th May 1972, p 16
5   David Halberstam, *The Making of a Quagmire*, Random House, New York, 1965, p 42
6   Hilaire du Berrier, *Background to Betrayal: The Tragedy of Vietnam*, Western Islands, Belmont MA, 1965, p 71
7   Cf. *New York Times*, 14th May 1972, p 16

8   David Halberstam, op. cit. p 42

9   Hilaire du Berrier, op. cit. p 148

10 David Halberstam, op. cit. p 42

11 Cf. *New York Times,* 14th May 1972, p 16

12 Quoted by the *New York Herald Tribune* (European Edition), 27th August 1963, in Hilaire du Berrier, op. cit. p 183

13 Cf. Thomas L. Ahern Jr., C*IA and the House of Ngô: covert action in South Vietnam, 1954-1963 (Unclassified),* Center for the Study of Intelligence, Washington, 2000, p 22

14 Idem p 14

15 Quoted in Hilaire du Berrier, op. cit. p 127

16 Ibid.

17 Quoted in Hilaire du Berrier, op. cit. p 128

18 'Church-State in Vietnam,' *America,* 10th December 1955, in Hilaire du Berrier, op. cit. pp 128-129

19 Cf. Guérard des Lauriers, interview, *Sodalitium,* No. 13, March 1988, (French) pp 18-34, and (Spanish) [pp 2-17], p 10

20 Ibid.

21 Hilaire du Berrier, op. cit. p 147

22 Ibid.

23 Cf. Hilaire du Berrier, op. cit. p 147

24 Cf. *New York Times,* 14th May 1972, p 16

25 Cf. David Halberstam, op. cit. pp 25-26

26 Cf. Hilaire du Berrier, op. cit. p 176

27 David Halberstam, op. cit. p 54

28 Cf. *New York Times,* 14th May 1972, p 16

29 Cf. David Halberstam, op. cit. p 128

30 David Halberstam, op. cit. p 205

31 Cf. David Halberstam, op. cit. p 25

32 Idem p 30

33 Idem p 44

34 Cf. *New York Times,* 14th May 1972, p 16

35 Cf. David Halberstam, op. cit. p 45

36 David Halberstam, op. cit. p 43

37 Cf. James S. Olson and Randy Roberts, op. cit. p 99

38 Ngô-dinh-Thục, 'Misericordias Domini in Aeternum Cantabo': Autobiographie de Mgr. Pierre Martin Ngô-dinh-Thục, Archeveque de Hué [sic], *Einsicht* (Special Edition), Una Voce-Gruppe Maria, Munich, August 1982, p 23

39 Idem p 31

40 Hilaire du Berrier, op. cit. p 183

41 Idem p 184

42 James S. Olson and Randy Roberts, op. cit. p 64
43 Ibid.
44 Ngô-dinh-Thục, 1982, op. cit. p 29
45 Cf. *New York Times,* 14th May 1972, p 16
46 James S. Olson and Randy Roberts, op. cit. p 99
47 Ngô-dinh-Thục, 1982, op. cit. p 63
48 Ibid.
49 Cf. David Halberstam, op. cit. p 56
50 Hilaire du Berrier, op. cit. pp 121ff, p 148, and Cf. James S. Olson and Randy Roberts, op. cit. p 242
51 David Halberstam, op. cit. p 197
52 Idem p 33
53 Cf. David Halberstam, op. cit. p 66
54 David Halberstam, op. cit. p 195
55 Cf. Hilaire du Berrier, op. cit. pp 121ff, p 148, and Cf. James S. Olson and Randy Roberts, op. cit. p 99
56 Cf. James S. Olson and Randy Roberts, op. cit. p 99
57 *Paris Match,* 23rd November 1963, in Hilaire du Berrier, op. cit. pp 243-244
58 Ngô-dinh-Thục, 1982, op. cit. p 13
59 Cf. Hilaire du Berrier, op. cit. p 244
60 Hilaire du Berrier, op. cit. p 244
61 James S. Olson and Randy Roberts, op. cit. pp 100-101
62 David Halberstam, op. cit. p 201
63 Cf. David Halberstam, op. cit. p 196
64 Idem p 56
65 Idem p 197
66 Cf. James S. Olson and Randy Roberts, op. cit. p 101
67 Cf. David Halberstam, op. cit. p 195
68 Cf. James S. Olson and Randy Roberts, op. cit. p 101
69 Cf. David Halberstam, op. cit. p 199
70 Idem p 206
71 Idem p 204
72 Ngô-dinh-Thục, 'What's Really Going On in Vietnam,' *National Review,* 5th November 1963, p 388
73 Graham Greene quoted in David Halberstam, op. cit. p 200
74 Hilaire du Berrier, op. cit. p 129
75 Cf. David Halberstam, op. cit. p 202
76 Cf. James S. Olson and Randy Roberts, op. cit. p 101
77 Cf. David Halberstam, op. cit. p 75
78 *New York Times,* 14th May 1972, p 16
79 Cf. *New York Times,* 14th May 1972, p 16

[80]   James S. Olson and Randy Roberts, op. cit. p 101
[81]   Cf. *New York Times,* 14th May 1972, p 16
[82]   Ibid.
[83]   David Halberstam, op. cit. p 277
[84]   Cf. David Halberstam, op. cit. p 277
[85]   Ibid.
[86]   Cf. David Halberstam, op. cit. p 245
[87]   Ngô-dinh-Thục, 1982, op. cit. p 20

IV

CAPITULUM QUARTUM

'IT BEGINS IN HERESY AND ENDS IN HERESY'[1] — THE MAKING OF A REVOLUTION

The Ngôs had alienated both the Americans and their own disgruntled generals, who had so far exercised restraint as part of their partnership with the US. With the Americans distancing themselves from the regime, the South Vietnamese army was now free to begin plotting another coup attempt, this time with greater success.[2] The Vietnamese people were eager for an end to the violence and repression at any cost, and as soon as this popular support for a military coup became clear, the Ngôs were impotent. Confusion followed — it was unclear which army units remained loyal and which ones rebelled, but in practice the coup was unopposed. It was that fateful month of November 1963. In the midmorning of Saturday 2nd, Ngô-dinh-Diệm was overthrown and detained together with "his Rasputin-like brother and closest advisor"[3] Ngô-dinh-Nhu, about twenty hours after the coup had begun.[4] The two brothers had tried to flee, taking refuge in a church, but they were soon apprehended and bundled into an armored personnel carrier. Diệm was still the 'mandarin in a sharkskin suit,' but the famous suit was now crumpled and soiled with mud and sweat, and the mandarin inside it was sleepless, disheveled, and in shock. The vehicle headed towards the army General Staff HQ, but only the brothers' lifeless bodies arrived at the HQ — they were killed en route, bayoneted and shot. Reckless and headstrong to the end, it seems that Nhu in particular was frenziedly stabbed after trading insults with the guard.

Of all the brothers, eventually only Thục and Luyen escaped a violent death. Luyen was serving as ambassador in London and Thục had been summoned to Rome for the Second Vatican Council. Thục would never come to terms with what had happened.[5] He would never accept two things: that the Vietnamese people could have turned on any Vietnamese leader so savagely, since the Viet "is above all a patriot, whether communist or anti-communist";[6] and that his beloved brother Diệm could really have been so hated. In Thục's naiveté Diệm was the "father of the Republic";[7] exalted, revered, a mandarin, a good Catholic — as long as Thục was alive, the Ngô family delusion would live on. It was Thục's firm belief that the CIA had been behind the executions.[8] In fairness, mystery and rumor surrounded the assassinations; some even said that the brothers had committed suicide — unlikely, considering their personalities, their religion, and the state of their corpses.[9] One thing was for sure, the hated regime was over. That same night the nightclubs of Saigon reopened, and the *saïgonnais* populace danced again. Statues and images of Diệm were torn down. Some 20,000 political prisoners were released — the devoutly Catholic Ngôs had presided over a regime of illegal detention, torture, systematic degradation, punitive rape, and summary execution of their enemies.[10]

It was "the end of an era, the end of nine years of the Ngô-family government,"[11] David Halberstam announced. President Kennedy was disappointed by this ultimate collapse of the strategy adopted in Vietnam, but the debacle also revealed his own failure to understand the complexity of the situation.[12] Kennedy's administration had spent a billion dollars and deployed 16,000 military 'advisers' in Vietnam, and 108 American lives had already been lost. As increasing numbers of people began to question whether America should even be in Vietnam, Kennedy himself was assassinated, just 20 days after the Ngôs. As for Thục, it is disputed whether he fled to Rome before or after the executions of Diệm and Nhu.[13] Most sources agree that he departed in September 1963, in time for the start of the new Council session.[14] Madame Nhu was already wisely hiding in America.[15] The US State Department arranged for the Nhus' three children to be evacuated from Vietnam and join their uncle Thục in Rome.[16] Madame Nhu herself later settled in Italy as well.[17]

In Huế, Ngô-dinh-Cân was at first offered protection by the US, but then arrested by the Vietnamese authorities. Cân lived his life like a cross between a feudal Chinese warlord and John Gotti. His operatives shook down businessmen for party 'donations,' while his loyal police captains did the same among their men. Whenever he felt threatened, Cân spread terror by ordering mass arrests and summary executions.[18] One reporter described him as a "rural Rasputin in high-collar Mandarin robes who wenched and swindled lustily."[19] The Americans demanded at least that Cân's safety be guaranteed until a fair and transparent trial could be held — accordingly he was indeed kept safe, duly tried, and then shot by firing squad.[20] It is generally presumed that, had Thục been in Vietnam at the time, he would also have faced arrest and trial.[21] Thục blamed Cân's death on the CIA as well.[22] But would the CIA have had reason to actually kill the Ngôs? America had "committed itself fully to Vietnam, and placed its prestige in Southeast Asia at stake — and in the hands of the Ngô family."[23] The US's priority had always been to contain communism, not to proselytize in favor of gentlemanly politics. The Ngôs had created "a clumsy and heavy-handed"[24] police state,[25] impervious to outside advice. Instead of a safeguard against communism and a stable counterbalance to Ho-chi-Minh, the Ngôs had brought chaos, unrest, injustice, corruption, and violent repression. The US's priority had thus escalated to avoiding a full-scale unopposed communist takeover of Southeast Asia, and the Ngôs had still refused to step aside. Instead of a modern and sophisticated strategy to maintain the balance of power and influence, the Ngôs brought America to the brink of a conflict which would become tragically reminiscent of the carnage of the World Wars, and which would shape America's destiny for generations to come.

Thục for one would never witness the ravages of the Vietnam War on his homeland. In fact he would never see Vietnam again. His journey to Rome in September 1963 would be the last trip financed by the Vietnamese taxpayer, and it would effectively be his passage into permanent exile. The Second Vatican Council had officially opened in October 1962. In June 1963, John XXIII died, and his successor Paul VI immediately announced the continuation of the Council. Paul VI sought to define the Council as 'pastoral' — that is, reviewing the day-to-day practice of the Church — rather than 'dogmatic,' or addressing the theory and theology of the Church. Initially, Vatican II was not seen as a revolutionary or even entirely novel idea — it was widely seen as the belated completion of the First Vatican Council of nearly a century earlier, which had never been officially concluded.[26] The original push to have a Second Vatican Council is credited to conservative Cardinals Ruffini and Ottaviani, who had first suggested it to Pius XII.[27] The Council would be held in four general sessions — official meeting periods of approximately two months each — in 1962, 1963, 1964, and 1965. The real work of the Council was done in the preparatory sessions and working groups in between. Thục had attended the first general session in 1962 (the trip financed by Diệm's government) and then returned home the same as all the other diocesan bishops.

Neither Thục's nor any of the other 2,500 individual bishop's contributions in the general sessions of Vatican II should be overestimated. The fact that Thục was an *Arch*bishop, incidentally, counted for nothing — the representative of Acerenza in Italy, future Cardinal Corrado Ursi, with just 70,000 Catholics and 50 priests under him, was also called Archbishop — a historical anomaly, not a rank. Nor should anything be inferred from the fact that Thục's brief speeches — to the symbolic general sessions — are publicly documented. The documented contributions, including Thục's, are mere representative statements — he is in fact reminded, within the record, to stick to generalities — and the real back-and-forth of Council debate went on behind closed doors. Assessment of Thục's positions at the Council tends to hang on whatever the assessor would like to prove — was he a defender of tradition or a liberal reformer? The record is rather inconclusive, and it does not show a distinct commitment in either direction. Thục did mention the participation of women both in the Council itself and in the Church in general; this was an ongoing issue during the debates and was later addressed concretely by the Council. It is true that at one point Thục may seem to be conjecturing for the possibility of women's ordination: "I shall be grateful to him who can present me with a plain apodictic text of the Gospel which excludes the sisters of the Blessed Virgin Mary from the sacred functions [i.e. the priesthood]."[28] But this statement must be understood in context; this was not said in the middle of a discussion or debate with a motion and a vote, this was a general session — the customary time and place for gentle provocation. Most Council fathers indulged in this type of good-natured hypothetical exposition and rhetoric.

Council fathers customarily tread on toes in order to make their points and elicit a reaction — similar to the verbal jousting which can be observed in the British Parliament. It may be admitted that Thục's rhetoric, provocation, and jousting does tend to go in the direction of the progressive rather than the conservative line, but such was the flavor of the Council. Thục also seemed to take a stand for dialogue with non-Christian religions, stating in Council session that "the absence of any invitations sent to the heads of the non-Christian religions"[29] was a 'scandal.' Again, this was not a debate, it was not a vote, and it was not even a discussion — once again, it was general session rhetoric. Claims that Thục was actually campaigning or 'pushing' for women priests or religious syncretism are exaggerations.[30] As for any possible behind-the-scenes interventions by Thục, we have no record. Archbishop Marcel Lefebvre evidently considered Thục to be one of the traditionalist old guard, and presumably he must have had some good reason for believing this, even though there is no public indication as to what this might have been. On the whole Thục's contribution was unremarkable; he did not vehemently oppose the ideology or tendency of the Council in any discernible way, and he duly signed his assent to the concluding Council documents — as did Lefebvre.

Thục's ecclesiastical outlook was hardly a clash with what would quickly become identified as progressive Vatican II thinking. His approach had always been "unanimity in dogmas of faith, but alongside diversity in areas that do not concern dogma."[31] In Huế, Thục had actually granted autonomy to individual parishes in matters of worship.[32] Thục experienced "disaffection"[33] with the liturgical reforms because he saw them as "invasive attempts to impose liturgical elements as Canon Law,"[34] which he felt the Vatican had no right to do — "is that not an abuse of power?"[35] — and which he felt clashed with the true tradition of diversity.

> "Jesus consecrated at the Last Supper according to the Jewish custom for Passover. Nowadays, the priest consecrates standing, and inclines to communicate. But why, since he [normally] eats sitting down? The Japanese eat seated on their heels; the Hindus eat seated on the ground, the food spread on banana leaves; the Chinese and the Viets eat with chopsticks. One could, logically, be surprised that Paul VI condemns those who celebrate in a different way, for example according to the liturgy of St. Pius V. He could, with that logic, condemn the First Mass celebrated by Jesus… ."[36]

Thục seemed to applaud Vatican II's endorsement of diversity: "diversity is [now] officially preached for incidental things and unity only in the essential things. The Japanese and Indian hierarchies are encouraged to adapt the Mass to their national characteristics."[37] Only the old Latin Mass of St. Pius V was prohibited, Thục lamented. He said that any blocking of diversity was not only unjust but also inept, in that the Vatican "does not dare apply the same prohibition to not only the oriental liturgies, but neither on the Milanese liturgies of St. Ambrose, [or] the Dominican, Mozarabic and Lyon liturgies. Could it be that in making this respectful observation, I have been instinctively driven by the Viet mania for independence?"[38]

Unlike the other bishops, Thục remained in Rome throughout the remaining Council years — he had little choice. When the

Council ended in December 1965 it became clear that he could not go back to Vietnam — neither the Vietnamese, nor the American, nor the Vatican authorities permitted it. But Thục was cut off from Vietnam in other senses too — he lost all access to his previously lucrative timber, rubber, coconut palm, and real estate businesses. What money he had brought with him, and what the Vietnamese congregation in Rome could donate, kept him from destitution.[39] He found lodgings in a succession of places — first in a Roman parish, then at the Cistercian Abbey of Casamari, and later in the town of Arpino, the latter two both in Frosinone Province near Rome. In Arpino particularly he could engage in light pastoral work, while "for the most part [he] was treated as an outcast by the Vatican."[40]

There was another kind of 'disaffection' settling in after the close of the Second Vatican Council, which would come to be referred to as the 'traditionalist backlash.' Archbishop George Dwyer of Birmingham (England) pointed out that "There has never been a General Council of the Church which has not been followed by a crisis of Faith for some part of the people, and even by a schism."[41] A considerable but heterogeneous sector of the Church began to highlight issues such as the perceived excessive or even heretical nature of the reforms and the perceived corruption of the liturgy. Negative reactions to the Council would vary enormously in depth and intensity, ranging from wishing to defend conservative liturgical tastes to rejecting the Council outright as a heretical Modernist revolution. Thục later wrote: "my few interventions [at Vatican II] were aimed at defending the Church of Christ against Modernist attacks, against the degradation of the Church,"[42] but this may be a case of Thục combining hindsight with wishful thinking — there is, at least, no record of any such interventions. By the time Thục wrote those words, the debate about Vatican II had taken new turns — the Council, it was suggested, had been hijacked by Modernists — and Thục appears to be simply echoing the language of anti-Modernist protest. It is clear that to interpret Thục's contribution to Vatican II as 'defending the Church against

Modernism' is baseless. But the crisis itself was real and is still ongoing today.

The disquiet was most visibly personified by Archbishop Marcel Lefebvre, who openly blamed Catholics' unease and discord on Vatican II, which he said "begins in heresy and ends in heresy."[43] Archbishop George Dwyer wrote that "General Councils are summoned to deal with crises, they are not the cause of them. Those who attribute the present crisis to Vatican II were reasonably answered by one who said that if the Council had not been held the crisis now would be much worse."[44] Rejecting this, Lefebvre drew a sharp distinction between the Eternal Rome of the pre-Council Catholic Church and "the Rome of the neo-Protestant trend" which had resulted from the Council reforms.[45] By the end of the sixties Archbishop Lefebvre was the most outspoken opponent of the reforms arising from Vatican II, or, as he simply called it, 'the Reform':

> "Born of liberalism and modernism, this Reform is poisoned through and through. It begins in heresy and ends in heresy even if not all its acts are formally heretical. Hence it is impossible for any informed and loyal Catholic to embrace this Reform or submit himself to it in any way soever."[46]

Lefebvre's positions gradually hardened with his founding of the SSPX — Priestly Fraternity of St. Pius X *(Fraternitas Sacerdotalis Sancti Pii X)* — and his traditionalist seminary at Écône, Switzerland, in 1970. The early seventies saw the Écône seminary and Lefebvre grow increasingly detached and alienated from the Vatican, as Lefebvre publicly and explicitly defied Paul VI in ordaining new traditionalist priests. Rallies of support and even church occupations ensued, in what Peter Hebblethwaite described as a period of "increasing virulence and relative success"[47] for the movement. Lefebvre was suspended *a divinis*. It was at the height of the crisis in 1974 that Archbishop Thục became associated with the SSPX, when he visited Écône to give a talk. It is not known how contact was first made, though it is obvious that Thục had recast himself as a firm traditionalist by that stage. It is fair to say that Lefebvre's positions were not always completely consistent either; he was capable of changing his mind and leaving his followers guessing. Later on, for example, SSPX priests were aware of a "notable shift in [Lefebvre's] 'line' after his old enemy Montini (Paul VI) died and was eventually succeeded in 1978 by John Paul II, who received the archbishop warmly."[48] But for now, Thục's position was clear — he was in the rebel traditionalist camp.

It was during Thục's post-Vatican II years in Rome that a specter came back to visit him from Huế.[49] Back in his days as diocesan bishop, Thục had noticed "sandy plots of land for sale at low prices"[50] in the Huế area. He acquired "several million Piasters"[51] from the government for the reforestation of the land, strictly speaking a loan to be gradually paid back over ten years. The priests of the diocese, in turn, could apply to Thục for a sub-loan. Most of the priests did put in for such loans from Thục, and the growth of wood for heating and cooking took off rapidly.[52] Even so, there remained a considerable excess of government money in Thục's hands — the remainder of the state loan which had not been given out in sub-loans to the priests. Thục used this excess to buy the land adjacent to his palace and had a large apartment building put up, renting out the rooms to government workers. He still had some money left to buy a coconut palm and wood plantation.[53] "Alas," Thục wrote, "Huế's destiny is to remain poor,"[54] because although everything seemed to be going extremely well, loan repayments to the government did not materialize. The blame was placed, somewhat predictably, on the Communists, who Thục claimed forbade the priests to repay their loans. Not everyone was convinced. By 1967 Huế was under the guidance of Archbishop Philippe Nguyên-kim-Diên, who had been standing-in *sede plena* for four years. Diên calculated that Thục had pocketed millions from the loans deal; Thục called this "an unthinkable accusation."[55]

The Holy Congregation for the Propagation of the Faith approached Thục about the loans matter in late April 1967. Thục had just returned to Rome from Paris, where his niece Ngô-dình-Lệ-Thủy, the daughter of Nhu and Madame Nhu, had been killed in an automobile accident aged just 22. Thục protested that the loan title documents were stored in Huế and could be consulted; that the coconut palm and wood plantation was flourishing and still in the diocese's hands; that Archbishop Diên seemed happy to collect the rent for the apartment building; and that Archbishop Diên now lived in the very palace built by Thục.[56] Thục threatened to go public and take the case to the Roman Rota, pressing charges of slander. The Vatican suggested the matter be dropped providing Thục agree to finally resign in favor of Diên. Thục described his adversary Diên as

> "that excellent friend of Paul VI, the pope who forced me to resign before the legal term so that Msgr. Diên could be nominated Archbishop of Huế, and could put into practice his policy of reaching out to the communists in order to undermine the government of Saigon. And Msgr. Diên used millions of my own money, without asking for permission … [sic]".[57]

Diên was not, it is true, considered a fervent anti-communist at that point, but he later became highly critical of the Communist government and pro-active in support of fellow Catholics. Diên's opposition to state interference saw him placed under surveillance, ultimately spending the final four years of his life under house arrest. But the situation was additionally embarrassing because, at the time the financial irregularities surfaced, April 1967, Thục's nephew Nguyễn-van-Thuận was nominated Bishop of Nha Trang, and Diên was to be one of the co-consecrators. Thục resigned as requested, and the loans matter was duly dropped, but his branding as an outcast was now assured.[58] Thục continued assisting in a Rome parish before falling out with the parish priest. Next he found a welcome at a Cistercian Abbey not far from Rome, at Casamari (which Thục mistakenly called "Calamari"[59]). He spent fifteen 'heavenly' months in Casamari, but again fell out with his hosts:

"I had been out on personal business in Rome; on my return I noticed at once that something had changed. The Father Abbot was absent. No sooner was I in my room than I saw the prior coming my way, looking worried, his face full of sadness; he told me that I, in the shortest possible time, had to leave Casamari and find other lodgings. Why this expulsion? The Prior said to me, 'The Father Abbot has been informed that you reported to the Vatican that an exhibition of nudes was to be held in the hall of the Abbey library, and the Abbot has been reprimanded by the Most Reverend Abbot Sighard, the highest authority of the Cistercian Order.'"[60]

It was true. Thục had written to Sighard — confidentially — on the pretext of warning him that a postulant at Casamari had expressed offense at the forthcoming art exhibition; Thục intended to distance himself from the whole thing in case there were repercussions. Nobody could blame Thục for wanting to avoid any further scandals, considering the year he had had. Thục's name appeared on the brochure of the exhibition as an honorary co-chair, and he wanted it on record that he did not organize the thing, which he found distasteful and "scandalous."[61] Thục had begged Sighard not to reveal the letter to the Father Abbot of Casamari, but he did. Thục was given a day to clear out his things. From Casamari he found a home in Arpino, a small nearby town, assisting at the parish church. Some peace at last, but this time Thục would abscond of his own accord, more or less, several years later. "That was the beginning of the final chapter of my life, which consists of nothing more than failures. Providential failures."[62]

Notes

[1] Marcel Lefebvre, *A Bishop Speaks – Writings and Addresses 1963-1975,* Scottish Una Voce, Edinburgh, 1979, p 190

[2] Cf. David Halberstam, *The Making of a Quagmire,* Random House, New York, 1965, pp 294ff

[3] Cf. *New York Times,* 14th May 1972, p 16

[4] Ibid

5   Cf. Anthony Cekada (as 'Peregrinus'), 'Two Bishops in Every Garage' in Clarence Kelly, *The Sacred and The Profane,* Seminary Press, Round Top NY, 1997, Appendix B [pp 287-319] p 297. *nb* taken from *The Roman Catholic* No. 12, Fall-Winter 1992, [pp 16-32]

6   Ngô-dinh-Thục, 'Misericordias Domini in Aeternum Cantabo': Autobiographie de Mgr. Pierre Martin Ngô-dinh-Thục, Archeveque de Huế [sic], *Einsicht* (Special Edition), Una Voce-Gruppe Maria, Munich, August 1982, p 9

7   Idem, p 13

8   Ibid.

9   Cf. James S. Olson and Randy Roberts, *Where the Domino Fell: America and Vietnam 1945 to 1990,* St. Martin's Press, New York, 1991, p 106

10   Cf. A.J. Langguth, *Our Vietnam: The War 1954-1975,* Simon & Schuster, New York, 2000, p 258

11   David Halberstam, op. cit. 1965, p 298

12   Cf. James S. Olson and Randy Roberts, op. cit. 1991, p 106

13   Ibid.

14   Cf. Spencer C. Tucker (ed), *The Encyclopedia of the Vietnam War, a Political, Social, and Military History,* ABC-CLIO, Santa Barbara CA, 2011, p 813

15   Cf. A.J. Langguth, op. cit. p 258

16   Ibid.

17   Cf. *New York Times,* 14th May 1972, p 16

18   Cf. Hilaire du Berrier, *Background to Betrayal: The Tragedy of Vietnam,* Western Islands, Belmont MA, 1965, p 147

19   *Time,* 1st May 1964, quoted in Hilaire du Berrier, *Background to Betrayal:* 1965, p 147

20   Cf. A.J. Langguth, op. cit. 2000, p 258

21   Cf. Ngô-dinh-Thục, op. cit. 1982, p 78

22   Idem, p 13

23   David Halberstam, op. cit. 1965, p 33

24   Idem, p 195

25   Idem, p 66

26   Cf. Paul Lakeland, *Church – Living Communion,* Liturgical Press, Collegeville MN, 2009, p 13

27   Cf. Michael Walsh, 'The Religious Ferment of the Sixties' in Hugh McLeod (ed), *History of Christianity Volume 9, World Christianities c. 1914 – c. 2000,* Cambridge University Press, Cambridge, 2006, [pp 304-322] pp 307-308

28   Acta Synodalia Sacrosancti Concilii Oecumenici Vaticani II, Vol. II, Part III, p 513

29 Acta Synodalia Sacrosancti Concilii Oecumenici Vaticani II, Vol. II, Part I, p 359

30 Cf. Magnus Lundberg, *A Pope of their Own: El Palmar de Troya and the Palmarian Church,* Uppsala Studies in Church History 1, Uppsala University, Department of Theology, 2017, p 68

31 Ngô-dinh-Thục, op. cit. 1982, p 9

32 Idem, p 68

33 Idem, p 9

34 Ibid.

35 Ngô-dinh-Thục, op. cit. 1982, p 10

36 Ibid.

37 Ibid.

38 Ngô-dinh-Thục, op. cit. 1982, pp 10-11

39 Cf. Anthony Cekada 'Two Bishops in Every Garage' in Kelly, *The Sacred and The Profane,* p 291

40 Anthony Cekada 'Two Bishops in Every Garage' in Kelly, *The Sacred and The Profane,* p 291

41 Quoted in Yves Congar, *Challenge to the Church: The Case of Archbishop Lefebvre [la crise dans l'Eglise et Mgr Lefebvre],* Collins Liturgical Publications, London, 1977, p 6

42 Ngô-dinh-Thục, op. cit. 1982, p 77

43 Marcel Lefebvre, op. cit. 1979, p 190

44 In Yves Congar, op. cit. 1977, p 6

45 Marcel Lefebvre, 'Declaration' made to members of the SSPX, especially seminarians and professors of the International Seminary at Ecône, Switzerland, on 21st November 1974, in Lefebvre, op. cit. 1979, p 189

46 Marcel Lefebvre, 'Declaration,' 21st November 1974, in Lefebvre, op. cit. 1979, p 190

47 Peter Hebblethwaite, *The Runaway Church,* Collins Fount, Glasgow, 1978, p 242

48 Anthony Cekada, 'The Nine vs. Lefebvre – We Resist You To Your Face (2008): the story of our battle in court with Abp. Lefebvre and the Society of St. Pius X,' p 2, at www.traditionalmass.org – http://www.traditionalmass.org/images/articles/NineVLefebvre.pdf [accessed 10th June 2018]

49 Ngô-dinh-Thuc, op. cit. 1982, p 77

50 Idem, p 64

51 Ibid.

52 Cf. Ngô-dinh-Thục, op. cit. 1982, p 64

53 Cf. idem, p 65

54 Ngô-dinh-Thục, op. cit. 1982, p 65

55 Ibid.

56 Cf. Ngô-dinh-Thục, op. cit. 1982, p 65

[57] Ngô-dinh-Thục, op. cit. 1982, p 66
[58] Cf. Anthony Cekada 'Two Bishops in Every Garage' in Kelly, *The Sacred and The Profane,* p 291
[59] Ngô-dinh-Thục, op. cit. 1982, p 79
[60] Idem, p 83
[61] Idem, p 84
[62] Idem, p 79

V

CAPITULUM QUINTUM

'PROVIDENTIAL FAILURES'[1] —
THE MAKING OF A FARCE

On 17th February 1968, Monsignor Ngô-dinh-Thục officially resigned as Archbishop of Huế, and was given the honorary title of Archbishop of Bulla Regia (a historically very important but no-longer existing diocese). He had been absent from Huế, and Vietnam, for four and a half years, and he was now 70 years old. Under the circumstances it was clear that he would never be able to resume any kind of effective leadership of any diocese. But would the Vatican have wanted him to? The last few years of his tenure in Vinh Long and then Huế had been problematic and even embarrassing, with interference and manipulation in pursuing his career ambitions, ambivalence and complicity in the outrageous family dictatorship, endless business deals and questionable money-making schemes, and spending his overseas travel allowance on cars. Even in exile, accusations and irregularities followed him around. Thục was in abysmal standing; he was seen as an intriguer, a miser, a politicker, the archetypal éminence grise. The occasionally-heard conjecture that his episcopate was exemplary (or even just normal) is a willful denial of the evidence. He was of course also genuinely poor now and dependent on charity.

At this point in the story the scene shifts suddenly away from Thục and Rome, to southern Spain; a patch of land in the countryside named La Alcaparrosa, in a rural area called Palmar de Troya, on the outskirts of Utrera, near Seville. It is 30th March 1968, one month after Thục's resignation and retirement. Four young girls 'see' the Virgin Mary, Our Lady of Mount Carmel, in a lentisk[2] tree. The girls are called Ana García, Ana Aguilera, Rafaela Gordo and Josefa Guzmán.[3] In the typically warm and rainy Andalusian springtime, the leaves of the lentisk tree, and the surrounding wild tobacco plants, were apparently "damp and red,"[4] which can cause dizziness, nausea, and sometimes hallucinations — but in the excitement that ensued nobody had the poor taste to point this out. The nineteen-sixties saw a number of similar apparition events in Catholic countries — Garabandal in Spain, Ladeira do Pinheiro in Portugal, and 'Mamma Rosa' in Italy — like celestial rebukes to the permissive society and Vatican II. As soon as news broke of the lentisk tree apparition there was confusion, including over the exact number of girls and their names — some reports also list Rosario Salas Fernández and Josefa Gómez Hidalgo. Curious visitors and pilgrims flocked to El Palmar de Troya. The lady proprietor of the land tried to deny access at first;[5] after all, none of the horde of visitors had seen any further apparitions. "But the people … [kept] coming to Palmar, *just in case*."[6] Reporters Manuel Barrios and Maria Teresa Garrido recreated the scene:

"Santa María, Madre de Dios…

"Silence. The Virgin is here! And God! This is no joke."

The rain starts up again.

"— Put your umbrellas down, it is holy water."[7]

There is soon a regular throng of about 50 people, and a "makeshift altar, in the middle of the mud. … Rosary upon rosary is prayed. On reaching the *Gloria* there is profound reverence … The seers collapse in ecstasy."[8] Each event lasts up to half an hour. The miraculous shrine was already becoming part of the local economy — stalls, guides, and transport were soon being provided by neighbors.[9] This was the spring of 1968, and the rest of Europe was in chaos; protesting students waved Viet-cong flags in the streets of Rome and Paris, and the Sorbonne was occupied. One of the Sorbonne's alumni, Archbishop Thục, was now retired, tired, and worn out by controversies and tragedies; he must have felt in serious need of a vacation. One of the earliest published investigations into the Palmar de Troya drama states that Archbishop Thục, coincidentally, chose to go on a trip to Spain "purely for tourism"[10] when, finding himself in the vicinity of Seville, he heard about the miraculous events at Palmar de Troya and went to see for himself.[11] He is said to have believed in the apparitions instantly. (It is not stated whether he personally saw or heard anything of a supernatural nature.) He is then said to have returned to Palmar de Troya several times as a pilgrim.[12] This version is contradicted by Thục's later account, which states that he knew absolutely nothing about Palmar de Troya until seven years later.

One year on, in El Palmar de Troya, everyone had forgotten the original 'lentisk tree girls,' who were fortunately allowed to move on and lead normal lives. Two young men moved center stage: Clemente Domínguez Gómez and Manuel Alonso Corral were "ripe for becoming protagonists in the drama. ... Clemente — a youth of 23 — has been chosen by the Virgin as spokesperson for all celestial requirements. The men and women of Palmar believe him and follow him."[13] Clemente's spectacular trances, visions, and messages began to take place with such regularity and predictability that visitors could be guaranteed an unforgettable experience — "Thursdays: Miracle,"[14] as cynical reporters announced. Clemente's style was unassuming, and his voice was not braying, forceful, or impassioned, just "Andalusian ... familiar and confident." [15] People listened and obeyed. Among the Virgin's apparent commands was to found a monastery and church on the site of the visions. Pious benefactors soon contrived to make the Virgin's wish a reality. The following year, 1970, and again in 1972, the Archdiocese of Seville condemned the supposed visions and disassociated the Catholic Church from the Palmar affair.[16] The apparitions were disavowed and the faithful were prohibited from taking part in the events.[17] In these years, Clemente Domínguez and Manuel Alonso quit their jobs and focused all their time and energy into raising money and spreading the word. They secured significant international support, pleading in the name of true, unreformed Catholicism and traditional devotions to the Virgin — all as requested by Mary in person.

Meanwhile, the war in Vietnam was running its course. Thục's nephew, Bishop Nguyễn-van-Thuận, was appointed Coadjutor Archbishop of Saigon on 24th April 1975. Six days later, Saigon fell to the North Vietnamese Army. Thuận was not only regarded as a representative of the Catholic Church, but also, much worse, as a representative of the Ngô family regime; the last high-profile member of the family still in Vietnam. He was detained in a re-education camp for 13 years, nine of them in solitary confinement. The communist victory also put a definitive end to any hopes that Thục might have had of retrieving his real estate portfolio, his businesses, investments, and money. 1975 suddenly became cast as the pivotal year in Thục's life.

The Palmar de Troya group — or 'Palmarians' — could have remained just another unauthorized, if by now wealthy, fringe sect, but everything began to change on 6th December 1975. The Virgin Mary (speaking through Clemente, of course) stated: "It is time for some traditionalist bishop to come to this place, and raise the Church from the prostration it is enduring..."[18] Dominguez had already contacted Archbishop Marcel Lefebvre of the Society of St. Pius X sometime previously, to appeal for ordination for his new religious order, the Carmelites of the Holy Face. Lefebvre was not unsympathetic at first; he had dispatched three of his priests to Spain to investigate. One of these was the Swiss priest Canon Maurice Revaz, a professor at the SSPX seminary in Écône. Revaz had been kicked out of his original order — the Canons Regular of Great St. Bernard (CRB) — for disobedience. He had been teaching Canon Law at Écône when Archbishop Thục visited to give a talk.[19] What subsequently happened can be safely surmised: Maurice Revaz was impressed with Palmar de Troya. The Palmarians had by this time adhered to a theory that the real Paul VI was being held hostage in the Vatican and had been replaced by a doppelgänger, who was a mere puppet doing the bidding of an evil conspiracy of Cardinals and Modernists. Revaz happened to share this belief. Lefebvre, having none of this, lost interest in Palmar de Troya and vaguely suggested that someone with nothing to do, like Archbishop Thục, might be interested in helping them. Revaz, on the other hand, soon began to lose interest in Écône and latched on to the Palmarians full-time. Revaz, now ensconced at Palmar de Troya, assured Clemente that he could persuade Archbishop Ngô-dình-Thục, whom he had met about a year earlier, to come along.[20] Thục was at the parish church in Arpino, preparing a Christmas crib he had bought, when a car carrying a priest and two laypeople rolled up outside. It was almost lunchtime (which a cynic would say is a typical time in Italy for a priest to roll up) and Thục's thoughts were on the Christmas Mass he had agreed to celebrate for the parish.

"A priest appeared who I had met previously at Écône in Switzerland. He said straight out, 'Excellency, the Blessed Virgin sends me to bring you, right away, to the south of Spain, to render a service to her; my car is waiting for you at the door of the presbytery, and we will leave right away in order to be there by Christmas.'

"Stunned by this invitation, I said to him:

"'If it is a service requested by the Blessed Virgin I am ready to follow you to the end of the earth, but I have to warn the parish priest about Christmas Mass and prepare a small suitcase. Meanwhile, as it is nearly midday, go to the restaurant in the village and grab something to eat.'

"He answered me: 'There are three of us in the car and we have not a cent left, not even enough for a cup of coffee.' I retorted, "Go ahead, all three of you, I'll pay for your lunch.' That lunch came to 3000 Lire [$4.40, or $20 at 2018 prices]. (To get to Palmar da Troya I spent 50,000 Lire in gas and food [$73.30, or $340 at 2018 prices].)

"While they were eating and I was nibbling on a piece of bread, I called the sacristan, asking him to inform the priest about Christmas Mass, telling him that I was going to France immediately for urgent family business and that I would return immediately [sic] in several weeks."[21]

As Thục implied, it is generally supposed that it was the first he had heard of Palmar de Troya,[22] but he did not explain why he instantly felt the need to lie about where he was going. On 25th December 1975 at ten-twenty at night, Thục arrived in Palmar de Troya looking dishevelled, with none of the pomp and splendour they might have been hoping for from an Archbishop. "The truth is that the Vietnamese Archbishop turned up in El Palmar de Troya in old and tatty clothes, oriental style, in slippers, bespectacled, [but] with a kindly expression."[23] Next day, St. Stephen's Day Mass at the lentisk tree. As Mass ended, the following message from the Virgin was received:

"My dear children: today is a great day in Palmar de Troya.

"I have here the presence of a Successor of the Apostles. What more could you want, my most dear children! Are you not able to appreciate the greatness of Palmar de Troya and the level of greatness that has been achieved this day with the presence of a Bishop of the Church, celebrating the Holy Sacrifice of the Tridentine Latin Mass of St. Pius V.

"Oh, my most dear children, children of my Immaculate Heart! A great, joyful day. A whole Chorus of Angels surrounds you at this moment. The Angels are singing Glory to God! ...

"A Bishop of the Church celebrates Mass in this Sacred Place. Do you not understand the crisis the Church is living through at this time? A crisis of confusion, error, division, heresy, apostasy..."[24]

Thục had now heard the proof with his own ears. Instantly buying into Palmar de Troya, Thục, still in his slippers, seemed a "pintoresque character."[25] But this was no hallucinating schoolgirl, this was "a Catholic Archbishop, to all legal effects... (ecclesiastical, that is) [sic]."[26] The Palmar situation became alarming for Catholic Spain:

"With no canonical or cultural preparation beyond believing in the supposed apparitions of the Virgin Mary in the village, the Vietnamese Monsignor Pierre Martin Ngô-dình-Thục ... ordained, just like that, the following people as priests: Clemente Domínguez Gómez, supposed seer of El Palmar and several times stigmatized, Sevillian and one-time accountant before devoting himself to the 'new Carmel' foundation; Manuel Alonso Corral, Madrileño, lawyer, with qualifications in business management from ICADE; the Irishmen Francis Coll and Pablo [Paul] Fox, occupations unknown, and the French national Louis Moulins, street painter and sculptor."[27]

Having turned up broke, Thục "gave the devotees [of Palmar] the support they wanted." [28] Thục seems to have tried to put distance between himself and Palmar immediately after the priestly ordinations, but they came looking for him.[29] "On the 11th [of January], Monsignor Ngô consecrated as 'bishops' Clemente ... Manuel Alonso Corral, Camilo Estévez Puga, the Irishman Miguel Danelli [Michael Donnelly] and the American Francisco Bernardo Sandler."[30] The latter three were already properly ordained Catholic priests, from Spain, Ireland, and the USA respectively. The five consecrations took place "almost in an improvised fashion,"[31] the first reporters on the scene recorded later: "Everything had to be improvised. Miters were coarsely run-up, pieces cut out with scissors and hurriedly sewn together, along with all the other necessary sacred vestments."[32] Photographs of the event show the new bishops in conical wizard-style miters, made from some kind of shiny satiny material. "The consecrations were carried out, naturally, according to the rite of Trent. It was two o'clock in the morning under the cold, blue, starry night sky of the Utrera countryside."[33] Cardinal Archbishop José María Bueno y Monreal of Seville once again vehemently condemned the affair, having tried to intercept Thục to dissuade him from carrying out the ordinations. "I know what I am doing" was Thục's response, "My conscience is clear and I am a Doctor of [Canon] Law."[34] Regarding Canon Law, for the record, here are the relevant delicts, described in the contents of a CDF (Congregation for the Doctrine of the Faith) document and reproduced in *Civiltà Cattolica,* 20th November 1976.[35]

"Can. 955, regarding priestly ordinations, requires that the candidate be ordained by his own bishop or, on obtaining legitimate letters dimissorial, by another. In this case the canon not only was not respected in any way, but in fact for two of the ordinands there was an express prohibition by their legitimate Ordinary [bishop], the Archbishop of Seville.

"Can. 953, regarding, on the other hand, episcopal consecrations, declares that these are reserved to the Roman Pontiff: it stipulates that no bishop can licitly confer this order, unless furnished with pontifical mandate. This canon was violated both in the consecration of the first five, on 11th January 1976, and in the subsequent episcopal consecrations ... ."

"[Underlining] the seriousness of this delict, in that in addition to constituting disobedience to the discipline of the Church it places its very unity in grave peril, it is affirmed that the Sacred Congregation for the Doctrine of the Faith issues [the document] by special mandate of the Supreme Pontiff."[36]

As to the penalties incurred, they were as follows:

"— suspension ipso jure, as per can. 2370, imposed upon bishops who minister and co-minister episcopal consecrations conferred without apostolic mandate, in addition to priests assisting the consecrating bishop and the subject receiving the consecration;

"— suspension ipso facto for one year, reserved to the Holy See, in accordance with can. 2373 (consisting of the prohibition to confer Holy Orders), imposed upon the bishop who ordains a candidate without letters dimissorial from his own Ordinary [bishop];

"— the sanction provided for in the year 1951 by this same dicastery, according to which a bishop of whatever rite or dignity who consecrates a bishop nor nominated nor expressly confirmed by the Apostolic See, and whoever receives that consecration, even if coerced by grave fear, incur excommunication reserved in a most special way to the Holy See;

"— suspension ipso facto from the order received, by order of can. 2374, for all those who maliciously accede to priestly ordination without or with false letters dimissorial. The 'malice' required in order to incur this censure seems evident in this case and, in any case, in the external forum it is impossible not to presume it;

"— irregularity ex delicto described in can. 985 / 7 for all those who, either lacking a Holy Order or for whatever reason suspended from it, may have exercised functions pertaining to that order, which are reserved to ordained clerics."[37]

As far as the validity of the consecrations is concerned, the Vatican customarily does not make sweeping proclamations on this matter. There are several fairly obvious reasons for this, the simplest one being that each ordination or consecration (each sacrament administered) is a single act which would need to be individually assessed as to its validity. Neither validity nor invalidity 'migrates' from one consecration to another. It would therefore be impossible or at least irresponsible to say, when there are such unusual factors in play, that all of the ordinations descending from Bishop X are invalid or valid. The Church asserts that there is a presumption of validity for 'regularly' (normally) conferred sacraments devoid of unusual factors, such as taking place in a field at two o'clock in the morning with hastily cut-out satin wizard hats. This is because under normal circumstances all the required elements are rigorously, consistently, and publicly monitored and assured. However, while refraining from casting judgment on the theological validity of these ordinations, the Church in these cases does tend to point out that theological validity is not the only thing that 'makes' a priest or bishop. Without canonical (institutional) recognition, even a technically 'valid' ordination would have no 'value.' Does it sound like a paradox?

"[Without] going into the problem of the validity of the ordinations conferred at El Palmar de Troya ... it is necessary to declare formally that the Church does not recognize, nor will it recognize in the future, any value to the aforementioned ordinations. Consequently the persons thus ordained are considered by the Church, to all juridical effects, to be in the same canonical state as before these irregular ordinations; meanwhile the canonical sanctions listed above, until repentance, remain in force." [38]

"The severity with which the Church handles such cases cannot and must not be judged excessive, considering the seriousness of the abuses committed and the situation of schism that could be unleashed. Nevertheless, the Church at all times keeps the door open to reconciliation, is given to mercy and forgiveness, should the persons concerned sincerely repent, desisting from their contumacy and making reparation for the harm caused, insofar as it is dependent upon this."[39]

Regular, official ordination carries a canonical status — a status recognized in Canon Law — and without this change in canonical status the subject does not become a priest or bishop upon receiving the ordination; they become what they already are, a layman, albeit now a layman who has received an irregular, illicit sacrament. The subtlety of this distinction understandably elicits blank looks from those uninitiated in the wonders of Canon Law. Spanish canonists summed it up as "a tenuous probability"[40] of validity, given the pervading mystery and insufficient evidence of requirements met.[41] Canon Law paled into insignificance for the Palmar bishops, however — this was now officially seen as the start of a new church. The Palmar bishops claimed that the Roman Church was the one in schism with them.[42] Within a short time, of course, Clemente and the other bishops went on to consecrate — first a dozen, then dozens of — bishops. On 24th January the *Triunfo* of Seville carried a story 'Become a Bishop in 10 days.'[43] Second-in-command Manuel Alonso defended the new congregation in somewhat vague terms: "The thing is that in the modern churches they do not pray … and the world needs a lot of prayers.'[44]

Meanwhile Thục vanished. Spanish reporters had no way of contacting him. They presumed he was being kept in one the houses owned by the new religious order, which Thục himself had endorsed in the founding documents, also declaring that he was now stepping aside to let them get on with it. It is impossible to state precisely what kind of pressures he was subject to. By the time the Congregation for the Doctrine of the Faith (CDF) published its findings, Thục had already returned — spiritually and physically — to Rome:

"It is hereby made known that, having acknowledged the repentance of Mgr. Pietro Martino [sic] Ngô-dinh-Thục, the Sacred Congregation, which released the decree of 17th September 1976, has already absolved said prelate from the excommunication which he had incurred, while the suspension *ab ordinibus conferendis* [of the Holy Orders he conferred] remains in place."[45]

Meanwhile the Palmarians went into their next phase, building a vast cathedral designed to rival St. Peter's, now replete with cardinals and bishops. When Paul VI died, Clemente was told in a vision that he was now the pope, and that the See of Peter had been mystically transplanted to Palmar de Troya. Clemente thus alienated his more level-headed followers, losing about half of them. More innovations were forthcoming: radical liturgical reform, a new version of the bible, and many canonizations, including of Francisco Franco and Adolf Hitler. Not all the Palmarians' followers deserted them and there remained secretive satellite groups in several countries. Their apparently plentiful sources of finance, considerable property ownership, and lavish pontifical ceremonies continued to fascinate outside observers.

Archbishop Thục's defenders have tended to gloss over the Palmar period and Thục's significant role in it. Even traditionalist and sedevacantist Catholics who do not wholly support Thục's later actions seem to tacitly agree that it is not helpful to the cause to acknowledge the Thục-Palmar role in the genesis of traditionalist Catholicism and sedevacantism. What happened to Thục? Why did he allow himself to be drawn into the Palmar de Troya business and, worse, consecrate the Palmarians as bishops? Some sources say that Thục was assured that the Holy See had secretly approved the consecrations and ordinations.[46] Thục, however, would have known that only the local Ordinary, the Cardinal Archbishop of Seville, would have been able to give the go-ahead, and he strenuously forbade it.[47] Other observers point to the tactics of persuasion used upon Thục — summoned by a message from the Virgin Mary, coming via a credible priest whom he knew, and who had held positions of responsibility. The language employed once he arrived, weary and disheveled, at Palmar de Troya, seemed to mix flattery and guilt. The messages eulogized him as a 'Successor of the Apostles,' a 'Doctor of the Church,' a 'Venerable

Archbishop,' while his cooperation was sought 'if you accept God's will,' to 'offer this small service,' because 'you are still able to render valuable service to save the Church.' "They manipulated an elderly archbishop,"[48] Spanish canonists concluded, denouncing the "atmosphere of crude infantilism and decrepit senility in which the ordinations of Palmar took place."[49] This leads to the unavoidable question of whether Thục was mentally well: "he is so old and poor that his head cannot be functioning correctly. He is nuts,"[50] someone uncharitably commented at the time of the consecrations. A more tactful opinion stated that "advanced age could have affected his psychophysical state."[51] Clemente Domínguez Gómez responded admirably to this line of argument:

> "Between Monsignor Pierre Martin Ngô-dinh-Thục and the Supreme Pontiff Paul VI, in terms of age, there is only six days' difference. Therefore, if Monsignor [Thục] is nuts then the Pope might be nuts too."[52]

In the light of several comparable Marian apparitions happening in the 1960's and 1970's, for the most part taken extremely seriously by at least some senior Catholics, clergy as well as laypeople, perhaps not all the egg should land on Monsignor Thục's face. Palmar de Troya itself was not immediately dismissed by Archbishop Marcel Lefebvre, though it remains unclear how close he came to direct involvement before backing away.[53] It would be a mistake to underestimate the extent of the distress and confusion experienced by traditionalist-minded Catholics in the fallout of Vatican II. The idea of apparitions of the Virgin Mary recalls a bygone age, a time of unquestioned truths and clear dogmas, which many Catholics were left pining for by the changes of the sixties and seventies. The craze of the Palmar de Troya apparitions was insignificant compared, for example, to the currently ongoing phenomenon of Medjugorje in Bosnia-Herzegovina, with around one million pilgrims per year. It is not unfair to ask: How could a cultured and learned archbishop, a graduate of the Sorbonne, give a second thought to Palmar de Troya and not dismiss it instantly? But was

Thục's reason not fundamentally the same faith that still draws bishops, doctors, secretaries, athletes, musicians, architects, and people of all ages and backgrounds to Medjugorje every year?

Apart from his hands-on involvement with the complex world of Marian apparitions, Thục also joined a select band of rebellious twentieth-century bishops. They are the 'bishops irregular' or 'bishops at large' who have lent their ordaining, consecrating hands to the vast and sometimes shadowy movement known as Independent Catholicism. For a variety of reasons, a handful of Catholic bishops have spawned new, unofficial branches of the bishops' family tree or 'apostolic succession' — like Thục did at Palmar de Troya — accounting for the unofficial bishops and priests (mostly excommunicated) of countless modern-day micro-churches. Early twentieth-century examples of the phenomenon trace back to Arnold Harris Mathew, a former Dominican and diocesan priest who finagled his way to consecration as an Old Catholic bishop;[54] strictly *Roman* Catholic holy orders became widely available by any means after 1945, with the radical reformer Carlos Duarte Costa in Brazil;[55] Duarte Costa was aided and abetted by one of Thục's fellow Council Fathers of Vatican II (the only married one), Bishop Salomão Barbosa Ferraz. Another Council Father was Bishop Mario Renato Cornejo Radavero, who later became in-house consecrator and ordainer for a breakaway church in France; in a very limited sense, in the sedevacantist field, Bishop Alfredo Mendez came after Thục; and in recent decades Archbishop Emmanuel Milingo — now super-excommunicated — developed a prolific freelance ministry. Whatever criticisms can be made about Thục, he was not alone.

Notes

[1]   Ngô-dinh-Thục, 'Misericordias Domini in Aeternum Cantabo': Autobiographie de Mgr. Pierre Martin Ngô-dinh-Thục, Archeveque de Hué [sic], *Einsicht* (Special Edition), Una Voce-Gruppe Maria, Munich, August 1982, p 79

2   The lentisk (or mastic) tree (or bush) is a wide bushy Mediterranean tree which produces mastic gum or resin.

3   Cf. Manuel Barrios and Maria-Teresa Garrido-Conde, *El Apasionante Misterio del Palmar de Troya [The Thrilling Mystery of El Palmar de Troya]*, Editorial Planeta, Barcelona, 1977, p 19

4   Barrios and Garrido-Conde, op. cit. 1977, p 19

5   Cf. Barrios and Garrido-Conde, op. cit. 1977, p 19

6   Barrios and Garrido-Conde, op. cit. p 37

7   Ibid.

8   Ibid.

9   Cf. Barrios and Garrido-Conde, op. cit. 1977, p 37

10   Joaquín Gómez Burón and Antonio Martin Alonso, *El Enigma de El Palmar de Troya*, Editorial Personas, Barcelona, 1976, p 174

11   Ibid.

12   Burón and Alonso, op. cit. 1976, p 176

13   Barrios and Garrido-Conde, op. cit. 1977, p 37

14   Idem, p 43 — this is probably a cynical reference to the Garabandal apparitions which were pre-announced as due to take place on a Thursday, without specifying the month or year.

15   Barrios and Garrido-Conde, op. cit. 1977, p 42

16   Cf. Barrios and Garrido-Conde, op. cit. 1977, p 54

17   Cf. Giovanni Caprile SJ, 'Su alcune illegittime Ordinazioni Sacerdotali ed Episcopali' [Regarding some illegitimate Priestly and Episcopal Ordinations], (Cronaca Contemporanea – Vita della Chiesa) in *Civiltà Cattolica*, Year 127, Vol. IV, No. 3034, 20th November 1976, [pp 375-378] pp 375-376

18   Barrios and Garrido-Conde, op. cit. 1977, p 42

19   Cf. Giovanni Caprile SJ, op. cit. 1976, p 375 (2)

20   Cf. Magnus Lundberg, *A Pope of their Own: El Palmar de Troya and the Palmarian Church*, Uppsala Studies in Church History 1, Uppsala University, Department of Theology, 2017, p 69

21   Ngô-dinh-Thục, op. cit. 1982, pp 85-86

22   Cf. Giovanni Caprile SJ, op. cit. 1976, p 377

23   Burón and Alonso, op. cit. 1976, p 176 — the original Spanish text makes a play on words with the word *gafado* [bespectacled] having a slang meaning: someone who brings bad luck, a jinx. Defies translation.

24   Barrios and Garrido-Conde, op. cit. 1977, pp 42-43

25   Idem, p 43

26   Ibid.

27   Barrios and Garrido-Conde, op. cit. 1977, pp 43-44

28   Burón and Alonso, op. cit. 1976, p 176

29   Cf. Giovanni Caprile SJ, op. cit. 1976, p 377

[30] Barrios and Garrido-Conde, op. cit. 1977, p 44
[31] Burón and Alonso, op. cit. 1976, p 182
[32] Ibid.
[33] Ibid.
[34] Barrios and Garrido-Conde, op. cit. 1977, p 44
[35] Giovanni Caprile SJ, op. cit. 1976, pp 377-378
[36] Ibid.
[37] Giovanni Caprile SJ, op. cit. 1976, p 378
[38] Ibid.
[39] Giovanni Caprile SJ, op. cit. 1976, pp 377-378
[40] Quoted in Barrios and Garrido-Conde, op. cit. 1977, p 110
[41] Cf. quotes in Barrios and Garrido-Conde, op. cit. 1977, p 111
[42] Cf. Barrios and Garrido-Conde, op. cit. 1977, p 55
[43] Ibid.
[44] Quoted in Barrios and Garrido-Conde, op. cit. 1977, p 76
[45] Giovanni Caprile SJ, op. cit. 1976, p 378
[46] Cf. Giovanni Caprile SJ, op. cit. 1976, p 377
[47] Ibid.
[48] Fr. Antonio García Moral OP and Fr. José María Javierre quoted in Manuel Barrios and Maria-Teresa Garrido-Conde, 1977, p 109
[49] Quoted in Barrios and Garrido-Conde, op. cit. 1977, p 110
[50] Burón and Alonso, op. cit. 1976, p 176
[51] Barrios and Garrido-Conde, op. cit. 1977, p 45
[52] Burón and Alonso, op. cit. 1976, p 176. Actually Paul VI was ten days older than Thuc, not six.
[53] Cf. Magnus Lundberg, op. cit. 2017, pp 69-71
[54] Discussed at length in Peter F. Anson, *Bishops at Large,* Apocryphile Press, Berkeley CA, 2006
[55] See Edward Jarvis, *God, Land & Freedom: The True Story of I.C.A.B.,* Apocryphile Press, Berkeley CA, 2018

VI

SEXTUM CAPITULUM

'NON HABEMUS PAPAM'[1] —
THE MAKING OF A MOVEMENT

Even before the close of Vatican II the counter-reform movement
had begun to organize, starting with Fr. Gommar de Pauw's soon-
suppressed Catholic Traditionalist Movement in March 1965. Since
then, tension over the significance and implications of the Council
has become a defining feature across the whole spectrum of Catholic
opinion.[2] Just as strongly as traditionalists reject aspects of the
Council, progressives feel that the full implementation of Vatican
II is overdue, that it was thwarted or betrayed by conservative
forces and the Roman Curia.[3] "An intransigent minority," Joseph
A. Komonchak wrote, is believed to have "engaged in rearguard
actions at the Council and thus forced compromises to be introduced
into its texts,"[4] which could equally be said of both sides of the
debate. But it would be a mistake to imagine a clean two-way split,
with all the conservative forces lined up neatly behind Archbishop
Lefebvre and his Society of St. Pius X (SSPX) in a face-off with
the progressives. Though Lefebvre is quite fairly seen by all sides
as exemplifying the resistance to Vatican II,[5] his approach was just
one of several organized responses to the hated 'Reform.' It will
be worthwhile to explain the basic distinctions within the Council-
skeptic camp, to define conservative vs. traditionalist Catholics and
their responses to Vatican II:

a) *Conservative Catholics* are disturbed by some or many aspects of the Vatican II reforms, typically but not restricted to the liturgy and the extent of its renovation. They see the many problems in the Church today as arising from the unfaithful execution or corrupted development of the reforms, in tandem with and pandering to a general "moral flabbiness"[6] present in modern culture and society at large. They may think in terms of the Council having been hijacked, distorted, overstated, or that abstract conclusions were drawn from the Council, blotting out tradition. In a nutshell, the Church went too far with Vatican II, so the challenge is to reconcile it conservatively, balance it out with further reforms or counter-reforms, and gradually restore orthodoxy.

b) *Traditionalist Catholics* believe that there was something inherently wrong with Vatican II itself, of which the liturgy is emblematic and symptomatic. Problems in the Church today do not so much emanate from Vatican II; the Council was itself the synthesis, culmination, and enshrining of all the problems and errors. It is not appropriate, for traditionalists, to talk about the Council being derailed or distorted because a truly faithful interpretation of the Council in line with tradition is not possible. In a nutshell, Vatican II was a clear break with Catholic tradition, and the challenge is to deal with the implicit and explicit consequences.

What are the implicit and explicit consequences of Vatican II for Catholics, and what action must be taken? On these questions, the traditionalist camp is blighted by disagreement, discord, divisions and infighting.[7] The image of a uniform column of the true believers, marching with resolute expressions behind a standard-carrying Lefebvre, fades into the ether. For all of the traditionalist camp, Vatican II was disastrous, and the questions thrown up include the following: was it even a true Council — what are the criteria? What aspects of or types of Council teaching are binding on all Catholics? How do we respond to apparently contradictory teaching

— are there precedents in Church history? In themselves these are fairly open-and-shut questions, but there is nothing like throwing a pontiff among the pigeons to see real divisiveness take hold. Every strain of Catholic would have to agree with Karl Adam that "communion with Peter and the Roman church has been regarded from the earliest times as a fundamental necessity of the Catholic conscience,"[8] but the question of the Pope, rather than the question of the Papacy, is the increasingly hot topic among traditionalists. None of the recent popes have truly pleased traditionalists, to put it mildly, and the tendency to 'sit out' a particular Papacy, in the hope of having better luck next time, has spread. In the case of conservatives, they hold out for a pope who will be more like them socio-politically and also distance himself from Vatican II a little, like a Benedict XVI; in the case of some moderate traditionalists, they hope for the coming of a true old-school pope who, taking into account the growing strength of traditionalism, completely overturns the Vatican II reforms.

Objectively, the latter 'soft-line' traditionalist expectation is highly unrealistic. The former, the hope of the conservatives (for whom no traditionalist love is lost),[9] is by far the more likely scenario of the two. It seems especially likely considering the imminent explosion of Catholic numbers in theologically conservative churches such as the Democratic Republic of the Congo, Nigeria, and Uganda, which are even set to displace Poland and Spain in the rankings of top Catholic nations.[10] But for five decades there has never been any indication of an actual overturning of Vatican II. All the post-Vatican II popes have broadly been, to varying degrees, *pro*-Vatican II popes. Mainstream or progressive Catholics may not see it that way, as John Paul II and Benedict XVI could be seen to have repealed or in practice relativized elements of Council teaching. But neither of them came close to questioning the inherent worth or truth of Vatican II. They offered what conservative (not traditionalist) Catholics regarded as the stance of a true pope: a more faithfully tradition-oriented interpretation of an admittedly problematic Council.

For hardline traditionalists, this matter of a 'true' pope is not just figurative, it is fundamental. Their logic goes that a) since Vatican II taught heresy, and b) since a true pope cannot teach heresy, then c) the Vatican II-promoting popes were not true popes, or at the very least they were in some sense defective popes. There are some intricate and complex variations on this conclusion. Sedevacantists are the group of traditionalists who, rather than wavering, declare that St. Peter's Chair (*sede*) is currently vacant (*vacante*), just as is always the case upon the death of any pope, before a new (true) pope is elected. For most sedevacantists the start of this vacancy has been pushed back to the pre-Vatican II date of October 1958 when Pius XII died, because his successor John XXIII, the originator of the Second Vatican Council, already held some of the heretical positions developed within it. The task of the sedevacantist, therefore, lies in demonstrating the truth of a) and b) above, that Vatican II taught heresy and that this renders subsequent papal elections null and void (it is advisable to avoid the terms 'valid' and 'invalid' as these have specific meaning with regard to the sacraments, which is a different issue). Within the traditionalist camp, *non*-sedevacantist traditionalists are most likely to partly or wholly accept a), that Vatican II taught heresy, but mount various objections to b), that this logically concludes with the papal vacancy.[11]

John L. Allen wrote: "An old car commercial ran the tagline, 'This isn't your grandfather's Buick.' I would submit that what we're looking at today isn't your mom and dad's Catholic Church — and it may not even be your older sister's."[12] For the hardline traditionalist Allen's words are literally true: what we see today is not the Catholic Church experienced even by the last pre-Vatican II generation — effectively the generation born in the immediate postwar years. For the sedevacantists among the hardliners the ramifications of the papal vacancy are devastating, but they are not even the only ill. Vatican II, which sedevacantists conclude was a work of evil rather than just a goof-up, also produced a liturgical reform which results, they believe, in some sacraments being invalid. The 'interim' or hybrid rites used during the Council years and afterwards are also marked as suspect by sedevacantists. Crucially, for sedevacantists, this resulting invalidity includes the rite of episcopal consecration, meaning that no true bishops have been consecrated by the Vatican since 1968. The consequences of this would be that the whole worldwide Catholic Church is left with around a dozen validly consecrated bishops, those few living bishops consecrated before 1962. These include the centenarians Bernardino Piñera Carvallo of Chile (consecrated in 1961) and José de Jesús Pimiento Rodriguez of Colombia (consecrated in 1955). None of these surviving 'true' bishops are involved in sedevacantism however, the only clear espousal of sedevacantism by a recognized bishop coming from Archbishop Thục in 1982. This episcopal invalidity theory is highly contentious and could be seen as a self-serving or tactical stance on the part of sedevacantists, as it leaves their movement with practically the only remaining active and valid (though not officially recognized) bishops in the world.[13] Furthermore, according to the theory, no validly appointed cardinals survive from the pre-Vatican II era. This adds to the difficulty of electing a future true pope, if indeed there is to be one — serious sedevacantists do not usually take for granted or, wisely, issue predictions about how the popeless crisis is to be resolved. End-times conclusions are not unknown among sedevacantists, another sign of the diversity within the movement — one estimate calculated 160 possible theological variations of sedevacantism.[14]

Archbishop Ngô-dinh-Thục's first witting or unwitting involvement in the sedevacantist movement is not easy to date. At the time of Thục's arrival in Palmar de Troya, Spain, the Palmarians believed that there was a true living pope, Paul VI, but that he was locked in a dungeon at the Vatican and had been replaced by an imposter, a paid actor. This theory was not exclusive to Palmar de Troya. It must have soon become clear to Thục that the Palmarians were at least de facto of the opinion that a true pope was effectively not ruling — the term sedevacantist did not come into use until the nineteen-eighties. The Palmarians certainly rejected the Second Vatican Council in its entirety, though this stance was not exclusive to sedevacantists or Palmarians either. By December 1975 Thục had already visited Lefebvre's traditionalist École seminary and met its priests, including Father Revaz. Depending on what the mood was like at the time of Thục's visit (the mood at École was changeable, with and like Lefebvre), it is highly likely that he was exposed to the kind of views which logically led to sedevacantist-style conclusions. Revaz, for example, who befriended Thục on the occasion of his visit to École, was already converted to sedevacantism.

Who or what did Thục believe? Writing notes for his memoir in 1976, Thục called John XXIII a "very pious, very holy"[15] pope, and referred to Paul VI as the Holy Father. He clearly did not have a doubt that they were true popes at that time, and in fact he does not indicate this anywhere in his writing — until his 1982 public declaration.[16] In general, Thục's worldview was not traditionalist in the Catholic sense of the word. He was quintessentially an Asian Catholic, with a mixture of ancient oriental mysticism and hands-on missionary practicality. The pastoral culture he espoused was not so much characterized by "docility and obedience [and] reverence for the ordained,"[17] as is the case with the western traditionalist conception of priesthood — Thục was proud to have been at the forefront of encouraging dialogue with the laity, long before Vatican II.[18] It seems unlikely that Thục was ever completely convinced by Palmar de Troya either. If Thục had not already sufficiently distanced himself from the Palmarians, after 1978 there would definitely be no looking back. Within hours of the death of Paul VI, Clemente Domínguez announced that he had been made pope by direct heavenly intervention. Palmarian bishops — Thục's episcopal descendants — soon outnumbered the priests, and included boys aged 16 and 17. There were around 100 Palmarian cardinals alone.[19]

After the Palmar business and his excommunication become public knowledge, Thục chose to quit Arpino and transferred to Toulon, France, where he received help from a Vietnamese (Buddhist) family he knew. He found a very small room with kitchen and bathroom attached, and in time found the company of five cats who lived and slept alongside him.[20] Thục's fourteen-year Roman period was over, and his "vast financial holdings"[21] were a distant memory by now, but he was at least back in a French-speaking environment. It was in Toulon that Thục met a 56 year-old Frenchman called Jean Laborie — we do not know how or where. Nor do we know very much about Jean Laborie, except that he was born on 16th November 1919, and by his own account, he spent his early life doing manual labor, with no involvement in religion.[22] Starting at the age of 45 Laborie was quickly ordained priest and then bishop — twice — by renegade 'Old Catholic' bishops. In the 1960's he apparently discovered, after a lifetime of indifference to Catholicism, that he too lamented the reforms of Vatican II. He founded his own mini-church, called the Latin Catholic Church. Laborie by all accounts was affable, likeable, and kind. Thục was obviously endeared enough to consecrate Laborie bishop (Laborie's third consecration) on 8th February 1977 — Thục had been reconciled with the Vatican for less than a year. Laborie later ordained Luc Jouret, the leader of a sect which committed collective suicide in 1994. Laborie died in 1996.[23]

Further Thục consecrations are said to have followed around the time of Laborie, but not all can be substantiated. It was surely becoming easy to claim to have been consecrated by Thục. It is widely accepted that a Polish-Frenchman called Roger Jean-Marie Kozik was consecrated by Thục on 19th October 1978 (three days after the election of John Paul II). Kozik had been ordained priest at least three times; the first time by Jean Laborie in 1974, then by André Enos, and then once again in Palmar de Troya when he joined the Palmarian sect. With the Palmarians he was consecrated bishop by Manuel Alonso Corral in May 1977, before Domínguez's self-proclamation as pope. Kozik is nowadays the leader of the *Fraternité de Notre Dame,* with an active presence in various US locations. Kozik is considered by his community to be yet another miraculous seer and visionary. Meanwhile, Thục joined the Roman Catholic Bishop of Toulon in celebrating Mass — the revised, questionable, Vatican II Mass, that is, which even the affable former laborer Jean Laborie rejected — claiming in his defense that he only pretended to celebrate Mass or 'simulated' it, which is considered a grave sin.[24] Thục was certainly not personally committed to sedevacantism at that point.

Sedevacantism, and traditionalist Catholicism in general, offers a comprehensive worldview as well as an uncompromising self-view, impinging on such visible things as dress, speech, gestures, and personal habits. It is the old Catholic religion of certainties, with no 'fuzziness' or grey areas. "True faith," Robert Schreiter wrote, "chooses selected items to serve as boundary markers of who is in and who is out."[25] Schreiter argued that these markers are taken from Pius IX's *Syllabus of Errors*,[26] meaning that membership is defined by negative traits. American Catholics who feel dazed and overtaken by high-speed changes from the 1950's onwards have turned in significant numbers to conservative and traditionalist organizations and publications. Interest in Marian apparitions also remains strong. There they have found answers, and the old certainties have been reaffirmed. "Fixity of identity," Robert J.C. Young wrote, "is only sought in situations of instability and disruption, of conflict and change."[27] Whatever the explanation, the USA quickly became a vitally important powerbase for Lefebvre's organization, as indeed with the other official and unofficial representatives of conservative and traditionalist Catholicism. This includes, of course, what Joseph A. Komonchak described as "what one hopes is the extreme"[28] of traditionalism, sedevacantism. Sedevacantism in fact remains "for the most part only an American phenomenon,"[29] with some small pockets in France, Latin America, Italy, Germany, and the UK, approximately in that order. It is in America that Thục's later bishops made their presence felt and breathed life into the sedevacantist movement.

In the first half of the twentieth century, American Catholics were, according to Avery Dulles, "a model of docility and obedience … performing their personal religious duties with scrupulous care."[30] Discrimination against American Catholics was still a stark reality in the early twentieth century, and discreet and diligent were their watchwords. They felt "no personal obligation to take any initiative [and] were not very vocal or active in spreading the faith,"[31] in Dulles' opinion. The experience of the coming decades would change American Catholicism beyond recognition; the Depression and World War Two drew Italian, Polish, German, and Irish Americans together, and in and out of foxholes (with or without the aphoristic atheists). Catholics hailing from the shores of the Baltic, the Mediterranean, the Danube, and the Celtic Sea were finally consecrated as Americans first and foremost. By the onset of the Cold War and McCarthyism, Catholic immigrants from Europe were no longer the main targets of popular derision and contempt, and with the first Catholic in the White House things had come full circle — American Catholics were fully redeemed. Inside of a generation, once-docile American Catholics were now the innovators, pioneers, war heroes, world-changers; and Vatican II was to be the celebration of their coming of age.

It is against this backdrop that modern-day unofficial 'Independent Catholic' communities, both progressive and traditionalist, sprang up. Combined with the social upheavals of the 1960's, progressive Catholic organizations sprouted and spread. Movements of former priests and religious, often abandoning ministry in order to marry one another, arose in the hopeful atmosphere of Vatican II, expecting to eventually be brought into communion with Rome once more. But this anticipated Age of Aquarius did not come; for all the Council's permissiveness, progressive married priest groups remained out in the cold. Some of them set up alternative ecclesial-style structures and hierarchies, being consecrated as bishops by 'renegades' descending from the Brazilian Bishop Carlos Duarte Costa,[32] or later by Archbishop Emmanuel Milingo. They operate independently, citing the chronic shortage of priests as justification; they appeal to the *lex suprema* — the supreme maxim of the Church, which places the salvation of souls above all else. It is a supreme law that allows considerable room for wilful or convenient misuse; the fundamental idea is an enduring and powerful one.

But the newly-acquired freedom and self-confidence of American Catholics also applied to the traditionalist camp.

After Fr. Gommar de Pauw's initial work with the Catholic Traditionalist Movement in 1965, organized traditionalism took off as a branch of American Catholicism in its own right, and the earliest sedevacantist religious communities date from the late Sixties: the Order (later 'Congregation') of Mary Immaculate Queen (CMRI) and the Most Holy Family Monastery (MHFM). The latter was founded by Joseph Natale, a former (unsuccessful) applicant to the Benedictine order, who discovered 'gifts' of prophecy and visions.[33] Today, MHFM is probably the most isolated sedevacantist community, though also probably the most combative; they maintain not only that the Vatican II Catholic Church is in heresy but that all the other sedevacantists are going straight to Hell as well. The former, CMRI, is currently one of the most developed and functional sedevacantist groups, following tumultuous and scandalous early decades under yet another 'visionary and prophet,' Francis Schuckardt (who proclaimed himself pope). But the majority of currently prominent sedevacantists — bishops, priests, at least one other claimant to the papacy, and many laypeople — are ex-SSPX (Society of St. Pius X). They are often rueful of the SSPX, citing with disdain how Archbishop Lefebvre flip-flopped between sedevacantism and sellout. By the nineteen-eighties, Lefebvre and John Paul II were warming to each other, but Lefebvre followed this rapprochement with a tantalizing French tongue-twister: 'I do not say that the pope is not the pope, but nor do I say that one cannot say that the pope is not the pope.'[34] The ex-members testify to Lefebvre's volatility, openly calling Vatican II and John XXIII heretical one minute and then exploding into tirades when his followers drew the logical sedevacantist conclusions.

Inevitably, it seems, the SSPX produced sedevacantist offshoots. The SSPV — Society of Saint Pius V *(Societas Sacerdotalis Sancti Pii Quinti)* — began as an internal SSPX dispute at Oyster Bay Cove, Long Island. A number of hardline US members became concerned about what they perceived as Archbishop Lefebvre's increasing openness to dialogue with Rome. Lefebvre was making concessions to Rome, including accepting the 1962 'hybrid' Missal, accepting priests ordained in the new rite (considered invalid), and accepting marriage annulments issued by the Vatican II-reformed Church. The Archbishop flew in to Long Island to quash the rebellion, but the nine rebel priests left the SSPX having arrived at sedevacantist positions, which were outlawed by Lefebvre. A protracted nine-year legal battle ensued — real estate had been bought by parishioners loyal to the nine priests in some cases, and by the SSPX in others, and all were now divided. Furthermore, the split covered several US states, each with their own courts system to fight through. The outcome amounted to a more or less equal division of goods, though with a distinct advantage to the SSPV.

The Oyster Bay Cove community thus joined the very small number of sedevacantist groups which were properly organized by the mid-Eighties. These included a Franciscan-inspired community led by Father Louis Vezelis, a Franciscan missionary alienated from his order. But they all faced an uncertain future without the ministrations of a Catholic bishop. The American sedevacantist groups were about to begin gnawing at a long-running bone of contention: the question of Archbishop Thục. By around the mid-Eighties the movement had its terminology — sedevacantism and sedevacantist — but no bishops to perpetuate the movement. At this point bishops began to emerge and proliferate who claimed their credentials from apostolic succession at the hands of Ngô-dình-Thục. Some of these claims and bishops came into the US via Mexico. The Society of St. Pius V, also bishopless, made a determined and serious effort to investigate and evaluate this new blossoming hierarchy — it was the start of the controversy of the 'Thục bishops.'

At the beginning of the 1980's, Thục and his cats were still living in his tiny, cramped quarters in Toulon. He heard confessions at the local cathedral, sometimes joined the bishop for Mass, and secretly ordained and consecrated people in his little room. At this point Thục got to know two German sedevacantist laymen, Heller and

Hiller. They had been busy facilitating Mass-centers, launching a quite successful sedevacantist journal — *Einsicht* ('Insight') — and establishing an education center for the propagation of traditionalist Catholic ideas. Heller and Hiller were of the view that the crisis in the Church could be mitigated by increasing the number of 'faithful' bishops in the world, and with Thục's help they aimed to become the promulgators of this new hierarchy. Such was their conviction that *Einsicht* even defended the proliferation of bishops in Palmar de Troya, though without explaining what place the 16-year-old bishops would have in the post-crisis Catholic Church. In 1981 two priests from Mexico, who considered themselves to be traditionalist-oriented, made contact with Heller and Hiller, and wheels were put in motion to have Moisés Carmona Rivera (68) and Adolfo Zamora Hernández (70) consecrated as bishops. "I didn't know them,"[35] Thục said later;

> "There were two Germans, Heller and Hiller, who brought them to me and asked that I consecrate them. I had confidence in these two gentlemen because I knew Mr. Heller. He is a very fine person. I knew him because he asked me to confirm his little daughter and I had confirmed her. These Germans are very generous."[36]

At the request of the 'generous' German laymen, Thục consecrated the Mexican priests in his bedroom. The role of 'generosity' in Thục's later-life dealings remains an open question. There can be little doubt that Thục received material support from sources such as Heller and Hiller, and there is obviously nothing wrong with that in itself. But as the SSPV priests observed after visiting the Germans as part of their investigation, "it was Dr. Hiller himself who suggested that Thục [had] consecrated non-Catholics for money."[37] Hiller explained:

> "When you see, had seen, the personal situation [Thục was in,] it's not an exculpation from [sic] him absolutely, but it is an explanation. When you had seen the personal situation he left in Toulon, a lot of things would be clear.[38]

"You see, Thục was absolutely poor. He had nothing to live [on], quite nothing. He was living in a very small room in a small street in Toulon in the first floor, and he had a small room and, nearby, a kitchen and the toilet in the kitchen. And then he had had [sic] five cats with him and the cats lived every time in this rooms, [sic] the windows had been closed with ... with hangings. Because the cats probably would be, would not come back ... So, you can understand there is a very *triste* [depressing] atmosphere there."[39]

Then Fr. Clarence Kelly of the SSPV asked Hiller "What did he do with the cats? [...] When he said Mass, I mean?"[40] Hiller replied: "The cats ... around very ... But when other people were standing there the cats were excited. ... They were like children to him, and when he was lying on his sofa there, the cats were lying round him — sleeping."[41] Understandably, it was instantly difficult for traditionalists and sedevacantists, even bereft of bishops as they were, to envisage this poor old man and his 'Thục bishops' as the future and savior of the Church. Somewhat unconventionally, the Archdiocese of Acapulco stated that the head of the Vatican Congregation for Bishops, Cardinal Baggio, had even ruled the Mexican consecrations invalid.[42] The question of the Thục bishops remains a divisive one for traditionalists and sedevacantists.[43] Earlier in 1981, however, Thục had consecrated an arguably more credible bishop, again at the instigation of Heller and Hiller. Michel-Louis Guérard des Lauriers was a conservative Dominican priest, theologian, and mathematician, who had enjoyed a distinguished career teaching and writing. Guérard des Lauriers' traditionalist positions and rejection of the Vatican II reforms led to his marginalization from the mainstream theological community, and he ended up teaching at Lefebvre's SSPX seminary in Écône. When his theological position then shifted further into the realm of sedevacantism (though he had developed his own version of it), Guérard des Lauriers was also expelled from Écône. At the age of 82 and six months, he was one year and two weeks younger than Thục when the consecration took place on 7th May 1981. Based on Guérard des Lauriers' qualifications and experience, it could be argued that for the first and last time, Thục had finally consecrated a freelance bishop who, in ordinary circumstances, could have been considered a suitable candidate for episcopal consecration. Both Guérard des Lauriers and Moisés Carmona Rivera have left a considerable progeny of bishops, including the most active and able bishop proponents of sedevacantism, such as Bishops Daniel Dolan, Mark Pivarunas, and Donald Sanborn. Bishop Sanborn, however, had actually been part of the original, skeptical SSPV team which had flown to Germany to investigate and assess the Thục case. Their findings were as follows:

"(1) [Sacramental] validity could not be proved in the external forum.

"(2) Even if validity could be proved, we could have nothing to do with the Thục bishops or consecrations because they were too 'sordid.'

"(3) There must have been something seriously wrong with the mind of Archbishop Thục for him to have done all the 'bizarre' things he did. He must have been 'crazy.'"[44]

As the perceived crisis has become more and more protracted, aggravated, and practically worse from the sedevacantists' point of view, the bishopless situation has caused several previously Thục-skeptic sedevacantist priests, like Sanborn, to change their minds. The SSPV for its part has remained firm to the conclusions listed above. But the situation has brought out other aspects of the sedevacantists as well; today they tend to display impressive media proficiency in order to reach supporters spread out over vast areas, often with high-quality websites, downloads, links, audios, lectures, debates, merchandise, live Mass streaming, and a recording of the most recent episcopal consecration (February 2018, with all three consecrating bishops being descended from Archbishop Thục). Through necessity, perhaps, the breadth and quality of sedevacantist media and communications often outclass their mainstream Catholic counterparts.

The 1981 consecrations of one French and two Mexican priests elicited the predictable response from the Vatican's Congregation for the Doctrine of the Faith (CDF), who wrote to Thục deploring his actions and citing the same canons under which he was again excommunicated. The CDF's public declaration began by reiterating Thục's 1976 actions and excommunication. The CDF observed that back in 1976 Thục had quickly "requested and obtained absolution from the excommunication most specially reserved to the Holy See which he had incurred."[45] The letter also pointedly reminded Thục that he had sworn to desist from such actions in future.[46] But:

"It has now come to the knowledge of this Sacred Congregation that His Excellency Mons. Ngô-dinh-Thục, since the year 1981, has again ordained other priests contrary to the terms of canon 955. Moreover, what is still more serious, in the same year, disregarding canon 953, without pontifical mandate and canonical provision, he conferred episcopal ordination on the religious priest, M.-L. Guérard des Lauriers, O.P., of France, and on the priests Moises Carmona and Adolfo Zamora, of Mexican origin. Subsequently Moises Carmona in his turn conferred episcopal ordination on the Mexican priests Benigno Bravo and Roberto Martínez, and also on the American priest George Musey.

"Moreover, His Excellency Ngô-dinh-Thục wished to prove the legitimacy of his actions especially by the public declaration made by him in Munich on 25 February 1982 in which he asserted that 'the See of the Catholic Church at Rome was vacant' and therefore he as a bishop 'was doing everything so that the Catholic Church of Rome would continue for the eternal salvation of souls.'"[47]

The Vatican imposed exactly the same penalties, suspensions, and excommunications as it had in 1976, deliberately underlining the consistency and repetition of its actions. But there was an additional tone to the CDF's document, which suggests that they were aware of the potential appeal of the movement now underway in the US:

"Moreover, this Sacred Congregation deems it its duty earnestly to warn the faithful not to take part in or support in any way liturgical activities or initiatives and works of another kind which are promoted by those mentioned above."[48]

The Vatican's condemnation did not mention some of the latest episodes in the Thục saga. April 1982 possibly saw Thục consecrate Luigi Boni and Jean Roux, though these fall under the heading of unsubstantiated consecrations. "He might have consecrated as many as a dozen bishops," Magnus Lundberg wrote, "even if it is unclear whether all consecrations that have been reported really took place at all. Some of the documents presented in support of particular cases are clearly fabricated."[49] On 25th September 1982 Thục almost certainly consecrated Christian Marie Datessen in Toulon. Datessen had previously been consecrated by André Enos (part of the Jean Laborie / Roger Kozik circle); after his Thục consecration, Datessen in turn consecrated his former consecrator Enos for good measure. Clearly, when committing the sacrilege of duplicated consecrations, there is nothing like being on the safe side. But Thục was phlegmatic; as he had written in his memoir, published that year (1982), "Would a certain Paul of Tarsus have been, nowadays, excommunicated by a certain Peter, because he consecrated bishops without referring to Peter?"[50]

Nevertheless, Thục's activities in Toulon were no longer secret, and he was unlikely to be hearing any more confessions in the cathedral or welcomed to celebrate the New Mass with the bishop. It was time for another discreet Thục retreat. He took advantage of the fact that he now had a mini-following in the US and accepted an invitation from the breakaway Franciscan group led by Louis Vezelis to go stay with them. Vezelis had by that time been consecrated bishop by George Musey, Moisés Carmona Rivera, and Adolfo Zamora Hernández. "While some of these details are difficult to establish," Palmar expert Magnus Lundberg observed, "it is safe to say that the last decade in Archbishop Thục's life was eventful and bewildering."[51] Thục turned 86 in October 1983, the first of two birthdays he would celebrate in the US. Peter (Pierre) had already outlived his contemporary Paul (Paul VI) by five years.

He had breathed vitality into the fledgling movement known as sedevacantism, and his 'eventful' and controversial life was still making the news — not bad for 86 years old, Your Excellency, not bad at all.

Notes

1 'We have no pope' – from the title of an article by Fr. Casimir Puskorius, *'Non Habemus Papam (On the Election of Benedict XVI)'* at http://www. cmri.org/02-non-habemus-papem.shtml [accessed 6th June 2018]

2 Cf. Joseph A. Komonchak, 'Interpreting the Council – Catholic Attitudes toward Vatican II,' in Mary Jo Weaver and R. Scott Appleby (eds), *Being Right – Conservative Catholics in America,* Indiana University Press, Bloomington IN, 1995, [pp.17-36] pp 19-20

3 Cf. Ormond Rush, *Still Interpreting Vatican II – Some Hermeneutical Principles,* Paulist Press, New York / Mahwah NJ, 2004, p 58

4 Joseph A. Komonchak, op. cit. 1995, p 19

5 Cf. Ormond Rush, op. cit. 2004, p 58

6 Michael W. Cuneo, *The Smoke of Satan,* Johns Hopkins University Press, Baltimore, Maryland 1999, p 4

7 Cf. Michael W. Cuneo, op. cit. 1999, p 87

8 Karl Adam, *The Spirit of Catholicism,* Sheed & Ward, London, 1934, p 106

9 Cf. Michael W. Cuneo, op. cit. 1999, p 87

10 Cf. John L. Allen Jr., *The Future Church – How ten trends are revolutionizing the Catholic Church,* Image, New York, 2009, pp 18-19

11 See John Salza and Robert Siscoe's comprehensive catalog of traditionalist objections to sedevacantism, *True or False Pope? Refuting Sedevacantism and Other Modern Errors,* St. Thomas Aquinas Seminary Editions, Winona MN, 2015

12 John L. Allen Jr., op. cit. 2009, p 3

13 Cf. 'Dominicus,' 'Petit Catéchisme du Sédévacantisme,' *Le Sel de La Terre,* No. 79, Winter 2011-2012, [pp 36-47], p 42

14 Idem, p 39

15 Ngô-dinh-Thục, 'Misericordias Domini in Aeternum Cantabo': Autobiographie de Mgr. Pierre Martin Ngô-dinh-Thuc, Archeveque de Hué [sic], *Einsicht* (Special Edition), Una Voce-Gruppe Maria, Munich, August 1982, p 75

16 Cf. Ngô-dinh-Thục, 'Declaration,' *Einsicht,* Yr. 28, (Special Edition), April 1998 /2, Una Voce Group, Munich, pp 8-9

17 Avery Dulles, *The Resilient Church,* Gill and Macmillan, Dublin, 1978, p 9

18 Cf. Ngô-dinh-Thục, op. cit. 1982, p 71

19 Cf. Magnus Lundberg, *A Pope of their Own: El Palmar de Troya and the Palmarian Church,* Uppsala Studies in Church History 1, Uppsala University, Department of Theology, 2017, p 90

20 Cf. Clarence Kelly, *The Sacred and The Profane,* Seminary Press, Round Top NY, 1997, p 48

21 Cf. Anthony Cekada (as 'Peregrinus'), 'Two Bishops in Every Garage' in Clarence Kelly, *The Sacred and The Profane,* Seminary Press, Round Top NY, 1997, Appendix B [pp 287-319] p 297; *nb* taken from *The Roman Catholic* No. 12, Fall-Winter 1992, [pp 16-32]

22 Cf. Jean-Pierre Chantin (ed), *Les Marges du Christianisme: "sectes," dissidences, ésotérisme; Dictionnaire du monde religeux dans la France contemporaine 10,* Beauchesne, Paris, 2001, p 148

23 Idem, pp 148-149

24 Cf. Anthony Cekada (as 'Peregrinus'), op. cit. 1997, p 295

25 Robert J. Schreiter, *The New Catholicity: Theology between the Global and the Local,* Orbis, Maryknoll NY, 1997, p 22

26 Cf. Robert J. Schreiter, op. cit. 1997, p 22

27 Robert J.C. Young, *Colonial Desire: Hybridity in Theory, Culture & Race,* Routledge, London, 1995, p 4

28 Joseph A. Komonchak, op. cit. 1995, p 26

29 Mario Derksen, *'An Open Letter to Bishop Clarence Kelly on the "Thuc Bishops" and the errors in* The Sacred and the Profane,' Cincinnati OH, 8th January 2011, www.thucbishops.com [accessed 6th June 2018]

30 Avery Dulles, *The Resilient Church,* 1978, p 9

31 Ibid.

32 See Edward Jarvis, *God, Land & Freedom: The True Story of I.C.A.B.,* Apocryphile Press, Berkeley CA, 2018

33 Cf. Michael W. Cuneo, op. cit. 1999, pp 87-89

34 Cf. Anthony Cekada, 'The Nine vs. Lefebvre: We Resist You To Your Face — the story of our battle in court with Abp. Lefebvre and the Society of St. Pius X,' p 3 and note 4, on www.traditionalmass.org: http://www.traditionalmass.org/images/articles/NineVLefebvre.pdf [accessed 9th June 2018]

35 Quoted in Noel Barbara, 'The Episcopal Consecrations Conferred by His Excellency Archbishop Peter-Martin Ngo-dinh-Thuc,' *Fortes in Fide* No. 12, 1993, pp 36-37

36 Ibid.

37 Clarence Kelly, op. cit. 1997, p 47

38 Ibid.

[39] Quoted in Clarence Kelly, op. cit. 1997, p 48

[40] Ibid.

[41] Ibid.

[42] Cf. *Einsicht,* Yr. 13, No. 1, May 1983, Una Voce Group, Munich, p 34

[43] Cf. Anthony Cekada (as 'Peregrinus'), op. cit. 1997, p 295

[44] Clarence Kelly, op. cit. 1997, p 12

[45] Congregation for the Doctrine of the Faith (CDF), 12th March 1983, *L'Osservatore Romano*, English Edition, 18th April 1983, p 12

[46] Cf. *Einsicht,* Yr. 13, No. 1, May 1983, Una Voce Group, Munich, p 33

[47] CDF, 12th March 1983, *L'Osservatore Romano*, English Edition, 18th April 1983, p 12

[48] Ibid.

[49] Magnus Lundberg, op. cit. 2017, pp 74-75

[50] Ngô-dinh-Thục, op. cit. 1982, p 10

[51] Magnus Lundberg, op. cit. 2017, p 74

VII

SEPTIMUM CAPITULUM

'MISERICORDIAS DOMINI IN AETERNUM CANTABO'[1] — THE MAKING OF A DIGNIFIED EXIT

Right up to the end of his life Archbishop Thục continued to embody the Ngô family reputation for "bizarre eccentricities and paranoia."[2] But the Ngôs had always been oblivious to the chaos around them. Thục's machinations had brought about the Ngô regime, and the Ngô regime's machinations had brought about the Vietnam War. Ironically it was in an America still living in the fallout from the Vietnam experience that Thục sought refuge in 1983. After each one of his later-life blunders, Thục swiftly packed his bags and moved on: when complaints of his financial dealings reached the Vatican, he agreed to resign and abandoned Rome; the scandal over the 'nudes' letter then saw him forced to leave the Casamari Abbey; when the Palmarian incident became public he left Arpino and went to France; and when the 1981 consecrations came to light he prepared to flee Toulon. Over in Munich, Thục's benefactors Heller and Hiller were not left empty-handed by his impending final departure from Europe. They secured a valuable declaration from him — to date the only unequivocal sedevacantist pronouncement from a recognized bishop:

> "What is the state of the Catholic Church we see before us today?
> In Rome the 'Pope' John Paul II reigns surrounded by his cohort of
> Cardinals and numerous bishops and prelates. Beyond Rome, the

Catholic Church appears to flourish, with its bishops and priests — the number of Catholics is immense. Every day Mass is celebrated in countless churches, and on Sunday they fill up with vast numbers of the faithful, hearing Mass and receiving Communion.

"But, what is the state of the Catholic Church God sees before Him today? Do those Masses, weekdays and Sundays, which the faithful attend, really please God? Not at all, because that Mass is now the same for Catholics as for Protestants. For this reason it does not please God and it is invalid. The only Mass that pleases God is the Mass of St. Pius V, which is celebrated by a small number of priests and bishops, including me.

"Therefore, as far as is possible I will aim to open a seminary pleasing to God, for candidates to the priesthood.

"In addition to that 'Mass' which is displeasing to God, there are many other things which God rejects, for example priestly ordination, episcopal consecration, and the sacraments of confirmation and extreme unction.

"These 'priests,' furthermore, promote:

1. Modernism

2. False ecumenism

3. The worship of Man

4. The freedom to embrace any religion

5. The non-condemnation of heresies, the non-expulsion of heretics

"Therefore, as a bishop of the Holy Roman Catholic Church, I judge the Holy See of the Roman Catholic Church to be vacant, and it befalls me to do all that I can as a bishop to ensure that the Roman Catholic Church survives for the eternal salvation of souls.

Munich, 25th February 1982
(signed) Petrus Martinus Ngô-dinh- Thục
Archbishop"[3]

The document is neither revelatory, nor is it good theology. There can be little doubt that Thục's aim was simply to please his hosts and leave them a parting gift. He mentioned all of the key flagship ideas in order to back up the sedevacantist cause; the New Mass is invalid, so are the sacraments, and there is no pope. Thục's final paragraph, containing the statement of *sede vacante,* is *non sequitur*; the connections he makes between all of these statements are inexcusably flimsy, and only a sympathetic reader, already familiar with the sedevacantist arguments, could hope to piece together what he means with this pastiche. He most probably thought that he was writing what Heller and Hiller, and any sedevacantist layperson, would love to read from a Catholic bishop. Could he seriously have been intending to open a seminary, or was this an unsubtle nod to the need for a sedevacantist Lefebvre? It is a shame also that Thục did not take that final opportunity to publicly spell out his real grievances with the Catholic Church. For example, we know that he quite understandably resented the fact that his leading role in the establishment of Dalat University had by that time been consigned to the trash; he was completely overlooked during the university's anniversary celebrations. Thục had apparently been airbrushed out of the history of the Vietnamese Church:

"[The] Holy See sent a message of congratulations [to the university], and many speeches were given. Only the name of the University's founder was forgotten because his name is not pleasing to today's Vatican! All's well that ends well. I founded the university in order to obey the Vatican of the day. God helped me. All honor and glory to Him for all eternity. Amen."[4]

Thục decided to flee Toulon and Europe altogether after the news of his second excommunication broke — his activities in the small apartment would have been highly unwelcome revelations for the local Church. His first safe port of call was Munich — Heller's house, where he had already previously stayed while receiving medical treatment. From there he prepared his transfer to the US. But news of his new excommunication had also reached the press in America, where the sedevacantist movement had begun to gain significance. On 8th April 1983 the *New York Times* reported:

"The Roman Catholic Church has excommunicated for the second time a Vietnamese Archbishop for consecrating bishops without papal authority, the Vatican said today. The Archbishop, Pierre Martin Ngô-dinh-Thục, brother of the late President Ngô-dinh-Diệm of South Vietnam, was excommunicated along with six other followers of a Spaniard who says he is Pope Gregory XVII.

"The Vatican said Archbishop Thục, 85 years old, had been excommunicated and suspended from the priesthood because he consecrated three bishops — a French Dominican, M.L. Guérard des Lauriers, and two Mexican priests, Moise [sic] Carmona and Adolfo Zamora — in 1981 without papal authority. Archbishop Thục refused to recognize Pope John Paul II.

"Father Carmona later consecrated two more Mexican bishops, Beningno [sic] Bravo, and an American, Georges [sic] Musey, the Vatican said. All six were excommunicated and suspended from the priesthood.

"Archbishop Thục was previously excommunicated on Sept. 17, 1976, for consecrating priests in Spain but soon gained the Vatican's pardon."[5]

No doubt glad to escape the publicity, Thục was warmly welcomed at the sedevacantist Franciscan house in Rochester, New York, run by Louis Vezelis. Vezelis, who was not mentioned in the excommunication reports, had been consecrated bishop by George Musey and the two Mexicans, Carmona and Zamora. For the first time in many decades, Thục tried to settle in to religious community life. What about contacts outside of the Rochester convent? During this period Thục visited Mexico, courtesy of 'his' two Mexican bishops, from whom he had unconventionally extracted some kind of promise of fealty — a distinctly papal pretension perhaps. A Mexico-based sedevacantist group, the Trent Priestly Society (*Sociedad Sacerdotal Trento*), organized a conference at which Thục gave a well-received talk, but he was soon back in Rochester

NY. Up to that point, however, he had not yet had contact with anyone in the Vietnamese community in America. There were a significant number of refugees from Vietnam already in the US generally (especially in California and Texas), with a fair-sized community in New York. But as Tuan Hoang, who attended Mass celebrated by Thục, recalled, "it doesn't appear that Archbishop Thục mingled among Vietnamese much at all up to this point. ... At the same time, it's possible that some [Vietnamese] Catholics were ambivalent while [Vietnamese] non-Catholics were antipathetic towards the Ngô family after the events in 1963."[6] In any case, Thục's secluded convent life was about to be interrupted.

A Vietnamese priest resident in New York soon got wind of the fact that Thục was living in the state. He in turn informed Tran-dinh-Truong, a former South Vietnamese shipping magnate who had made millions as a contractor for the US military. Tran-dinh-Truong's actions during the Fall of Saigon have been the subject of debate, with Tran claiming that his 24 ships and hundreds of trucks aided the evacuation of thousands of South Vietnamese civilians and military. Tran himself traveled to the United States in one of his own ships, carrying two suitcases full of gold. He bought a string of hotels in New York City, including the Hotel Carter (allegedly dubbed 'America's dirtiest hotel') and the infamous Hotel Kenmore Hall, which was seized by the US Marshals Service because of its generally degenerate state and for being "a bizarre warehouse for crack dealers, prostitutes, robbers and extortionists."[7] With Tran's help, the news of Thục's presence made its way to Missouri, specifically to a refugee priest called Tran-van-Dien. Fr. Dien was a diocesan priest from Thục's former archdiocese of Huế, then living in retirement with the Vietnamese Congregation of the Blessed Mother Co-Redemptrix (the CMC, or *Congregatio Matris Coredemptricis,* in Latin). Gradually, dispersed members of Thục's old entourage were coming together for the "rescue and return"[8] of the old man. Fr. Dien wrote to one of Thục's most trusted former employees, then living in California, who agreed to approach the Archbishop. It was subsequently ascertained that a) Thục was indeed still in the embrace of the sedevacantists, b) he had cancer, c) he was keen to get away, and perhaps visit his old friends in California, but d) he was broke again.[9]

Fr. Dien was one of just two retired priests living at the CMC headquarters in Carthage, Missouri, the other being an actual CMC member. Once Fr. Dien had the full facts about Thục's situation, he was confident in approaching the CMC superior, Fr. Nguyen-duc-Thiep, about finding a solution. They agreed to get Thục out of the sedevacantist community in upstate New York and take care of him there in Southwestern Missouri:

> "Around the lunar New Year of the Rat, 1984, the retired priest Fr. Dien flew to New York and asked to visit Archbishop Thục then staying with the [sedevacantist] Franciscans … Fr. Dien invited Archbishop Thục to attend the New Year's ceremony organized by [the] Vietnamese [community] in Washington DC. The automobile took Fr. Dien, Fr. Thiep, Mr. Tran-dình-Truong, and Archbishop Thục. It stopped in New York City to pick up some items, then sped up to Washington [not to the Vietnamese event but] to the Apostolic Nunciature of the Holy See. The illicit Bishop Vezelis had sent a bodyguard to go with Archbishop Thục. Both sides fought and argued over Thục, and they called the police to intervene. The police declared that the Archbishop had the full right to choose his residence, and he loudly stated that he chose the Vietnamese community and the Roman Church."[10]

Bishop Vezelis, his Franciscans, and *Einsicht* magazine all referred to the event as an abduction;[11] later there was speculation that the Vietnamese priests had coerced, threatened, or even drugged Thục. The fact is that after the day's drama Archbishop Thục was still able to summon up the courage to spend the night at one of Mr. Truong's fine establishments (the Hotel Carter in New York City). He flew to Louisiana on 2nd February 1984 (New Year's Day, of the Lunar Year of the Rat) before heading to Carthage, Missouri, to see out his remaining days with the priests and brothers of the CMC. His reappearance among his fellow Vietnamese Catholics provided the refugees with a reassuring link to the past: "During the Vietnam conflict, northern Catholics that moved south provided a consistent anticommunist stand and support for Diệm when he was in power. They grieved gravely for Diệm after his death in 1963, and grieved a lot more after Saigon fell to the communists."[12] Now their fallen leader's flesh and blood was present for all to see, among them once more, in Carthage.

It was there, six months later, that Archbishop Thục had his swan song. It was the first weekend in August 1984, at a major gathering of the Vietnamese Catholic community. It was Thục's first and last high-profile public appearance since leaving Vietnam, and he was warmly received. The occasion was one of the annual 'Marian Days' weekends, which had begun in 1978 as an initiative of the CMC Headquarters in Carthage. It has since become one of the biggest Catholic events in the United States. A statue of the Virgin Mary giving comfort to Vietnamese refugees — Our Lady of Refugees — was erected at the Carthage HQ in 1983, and it has served as a rallying symbol for the annual gathering ever since. It also became a symbol of this wayward old cleric having finally and definitively returned to the bosom of the Roman Catholic Church. He presided at Mass alongside a visiting bishop from Vietnam and in the company of thousands of his country-folk. Fortunately, it seems that the Vietnamese Catholic community at large did not hold Thục's misdemeanors against him. Tuan Hoang was one of the attendees who appreciated seeing Archbishop Thục in the flesh.

> "[The] appearance of Archbishop Thục was something of a moral victory for the Catholic refugees in general and the CMC in particular. ... Thục's return [to the Church] carried double or even triple meaning to the Vietnamese. It was a return to the Vatican and the Church, yes, but also [a] return to Vietnamese Catholicism and, in some respects, [a] return to history. Catholicism, nationalism, and historical memory interacted considerably in this case."[13]

Perhaps Thục's biggest mistake had been to leave Vietnam in the first place; it is possible that he was correct in thinking that his escape saved his life, but what kind of a life did he have after

1963? Thục had praised Rome as his "spiritual and intellectual homeland,"[14] but his Catholicism always remained, as Tuan Hoang observed, Vietnamese Catholicism. He never truly took any other Catholic epithet seriously, whether Palmarian, Traditionalist, or even Roman, *sensus literalis*. Thục was the product of a Church in transformation — an increasingly third-world Church. Much had changed in a short time: the Vatican's consistories (the investitures of new cardinals) of 1953 and 1958 had included only one new Asian cardinal between them — Cardinal Gracias of Bombay — and no Africans, and the new cardinals of 1953 and 1958 had an average age of 64 and 68 respectively. In the 1960 consistory, however, three of the seven named cardinals were non-Europeans; two were Asian — Cardinal Doi of Tokyo and Cardinal Santos of Manila, who was aged only 51, and one was African — Cardinal Rugambwa of Tanzania, who was only 47. Since cardinals choose the pope, the choice of the cardinals determines the direction of the Church. At the conclave which elected Paul VI a quarter of the cardinals were from the third world or Eastern Europe, and by the time of the 1965 consistory nearly half of the newly-appointed cardinals were from the third world or Eastern Europe. The Church's worldview would be transformed totally and irreversibly.

The Church was rapidly becoming more third-world, more Asian, and more youthful. The last clutch of newly-appointed cardinals of the nineteen-fifties (December 1959) had an average age of 72, but by the end of Vatican II it had become normal to appoint cardinals in their mid-forties to early fifties — youth almost unheard of among cardinals in modern times, up until then that is. At Vatican II itself, Thục was by no means the oldest Council Father at 65, but he was a full three decades older than the youngest bishops. Bishop Mario Renato Cornejo Radavero of Peru, incidentally, exactly thirty years Thục's junior, would also become a kind of renegade, like Thục; he quit the Church to get married in 1969, and was taken in by a French traditionalist community, where he lives to this day (with his wife), consecrating priests and bishops for them. But progressive third world council fathers did not just hail from among the youngsters; consider the case of Salomão Barbosa Ferraz, nearly 18 years older than Thục, and the only married bishop (and father of seven) at Vatican II. In his native Brazil, Ferraz campaigned vigorously for the vernacular Mass (he had already started celebrating it himself, on his own initiative) and married priests (he had unofficially ordained many of them), and unification with Protestants (he frequently attended Protestant services).[15] Thục himself was entirely in line with the flow and tide of Vatican II, but then how many were not? Lefebvre still stands out, but even he signed the final council documents. It is reasonable and pertinent to ask whether Thục was progressive or conservative, but in reality he was neither. He was simply *tiers monde* — looking towards a third way; the third world way. The Council and the Church were turning towards the third world too. Thục's theology and outlook were quintessentially Southeast Asian, straddling the fine line between local character and syncretism; Christianity not challenging local ways of thinking but complementing them.

The unofficial or 'illicit' consecration of bishops connects the four very different bishops mentioned above — the Peruvian Cornejo Radavero, the Brazilian Ferraz, the French Lefebvre, and the Vietnamese Thục. They all consecrated bishops without that all important document, the papal mandate; actions which, with apparently varying motivations, highlighted different aspects of the same religious crisis. But were their motivations really that different? They were all affirming a kind of independence and a challenge to the established authorities. In the cases of Thục and Salomão Barbosa Ferraz particularly, they inadvertently contributed to the subculture of *episcopi vagantes,* a phenomenon which centers on the pursuit and acquisition of Holy Orders stemming *from* the Roman Catholic Church, but *outside* of the Roman Catholic Church. This is then thought to confer upon the individual a legitimate springboard from which to found their own church or community. This then results in a phenomenon of generally small or very small "micro-churches"[16] which are to varying degrees — and often debatably — Catholic in character or affinity. They may be progressive, traditionalist, or neither, and are usually led by at least one freelance bishop — "a most dangerous species."[17] The somewhat sinister-sounding term *episcopi vagantes,* meaning 'wandering bishops,' has alternated with more sympathetic terms such as "bishops extraordinary"[18] or "independent episcopacy."[19] This subculture is also referred to as 'Independent Catholicism'[20] or the 'Independent Sacramental Movement,'[21] while other authors just write them all off as schismatics.[22]

Previously, by far the most common source of ordination for this subculture of independent micro-churches were the various offshoots of the European Old Catholic movement, but these days Holy Orders connected to Ferraz, Thục, and the Brazilian Duarte Costa are at least as widespread.[23] Apart from the strange individual circumstances that have resulted in certain bishops ordaining 'left, right and center,' what can be said of this proliferation of splinter groups and freelance bishops, in such an ostensibly tight-knit organization as the Catholic Church? Not surprisingly, forward-thinking theologians after Vatican II foresaw something very similar in the Church's future, and they even welcomed it — this included the future conservative Joseph Ratzinger:

> "Maybe we are facing a new and different kind of epoch in the Church's history, where Christianity will again be characterized more by the mustard seed, where it will exist in small, seemingly insignificant groups that nonetheless live an intensive struggle against evil and bring the good into the world..."[24] "The Church ... will, biblically speaking, become the salt of the earth again."[25]

Yves Congar, writing about the Lefebvre case in 1976, called for "internal ecumenism" to address breakaway communities, which "should be less difficult than the other kind of ecumenism since we have many more points of reference in common. Indeed, we have (nearly) everything in common!"[26] In response to the danger of sectarianism presented by splinter groups, Avery Dulles wrote that Catholicism itself "may be expected to assume a 'sectarian' stance precisely in order to make a distinctively Catholic contribution."[27]

Only the sedevacantists' central tenet, the no-pope situation, really stands between them and the Vatican, when viewed from the Vatican's side. Apart from that sticking point, the modern Catholic Church is diverse enough and tolerant enough to potentially embrace them. Beyond the papal issue, furthermore, the numerous bishops who currently descend from Archbishop Thục are a very diverse bunch too — this includes of course the sedevacantists and Palmarians, but also some liberal 'Old Catholics' and other independent bishops.[28] There are also a number of independent bishops descending from the many bishops who have abandoned the Palmarian sect (such as former Pope Gregory XVIII, who left in order to get married in 2016). One such bishop famously ordained the Irish singer Sinéad O'Connor in 1999, though with highly questionable validity. It could be that the principal attraction of joining an Independent Catholic micro-church is not the theological or liturgical inclination that they subscribe to, but the opportunity to operate within more flexible boundaries and have easier access to leadership, sacraments, priesthood, and interesting people.

There have been other high-profile renegade bishops who have consecrated further bishops without authorization. These include Archbishop Emmanuel Milingo (who missed out on being a council father, as he was consecrated by Paul VI in 1969) and Bishop Alfredo Méndez González, who was consecrated in 1960 by Cardinal Spellman. It was to Bishop Alfredo Méndez that the Society of St. Pius V (SSPV) ultimately turned to solve the problem of finding a bishop and valid ordinations for the sedevacantists. Fr. Clarence Kelly of the SSPV (and ex-SSPX) held fast to the conclusions drawn after visiting those generous Germans, Hiller and Heller, and continues to reject the Thục bishops because

"(1) [Sacramental] [v]alidity could not be proved in the external forum.

"(2) Even if validity could be proved, we could have nothing to do with the Thục bishops or consecrations because they were too 'sordid.'

"(3) There must have been something seriously wrong with the mind of Archbishop Thục for him to have done all the 'bizarre' things he did. He must have been 'crazy.'"[29]

As the years passed, the original line-up of the SSPV itself, 'the nine' rebel sedevacantists who split from the SSPX, began to disintegrate. As the priests went their separate ways, some of them revisited the issue of the 'Thục bishops' with an open mind, and were now in favor of the Thục consecrations. Kelly and company, on the other hand, successfully made contact with Bishop Méndez, the retired bishop of Arecibo in Puerto Rico. Méndez agreed, first, to ordain priests for the SSPV, and then to consecrate Kelly as bishop, at Carlsbad, California, in 1993. Kelly's consecration came under heavy fire from other sedevacantists, for its perceived hypocrisy and secrecy (Bishop Méndez had stipulated the condition that the consecration only be made public after his death). In fairness, all of Thục's original consecrations were done in secret — in his Toulon bedroom, before an overwhelmingly feline congregation; he could hardly have asked to borrow Toulon Cathedral after all. As far as the local Church knew, Thục's ministry in retirement consisted of hearing confessions and assisting the bishop at Mass. And as for secrecy, Thục's Palmar consecrations took place in the middle of the night in a field in the Spanish countryside, in order to escape the watchful eyes of the local Cardinal Archbishop. The Thục camp retaliated that it was Méndez whose mind was slipping at the time of the consecration, jeopardizing validity, not Thục. There were additional debates arising from the suggestion of necessity or non-necessity of having witnesses to the various consecrations — priest witnesses, competent witnesses, qualified witnesses, whiskered witnesses, etc.

And so on; an unrelenting back-and-forth in defense and criticism of the Thục and Méndez consecrations. All of the consecrations — Palmar, Toulon, Carlsbad — have been subjected to challenges on the basis of defective form. Thục was believed to have cut parts out of the Palmar consecrations, and some said that they took place outside of Mass altogether. Bishop Méndez was said to have mispronounced a word of the Latin during an SSPV ordination. Thục was said to have fluffed or skipped parts of the rite in the Toulon consecrations. Pope Pius XII's *Sacramentum Ordinis* set out very minimal requirements for the sacramentally valid wording of a consecration, but there are limits. Since then, however, the current generations of sedevacantist bishops are most likely to not only ensure that the form and conduct of consecration ceremonies is public, witnessed, and videoed, but also that the entire rite is meticulously observed in its minutest details — three or four hours long in the case of an episcopal consecration. But attention to detail is not retroactive of course — if the original Thục (or Méndez) consecration/s, from which modern ones stem, were to be invalid, then all the subsequent consecrations would be too.

The official Catholic Church does not expend time and energy refuting validity in 'freelance bishop' cases, ever. In the absence of a glaring defect, such as the consecrating bishop not being a bishop to begin with, Canon Law traditionally presumes validity. With regard to such consecrations Canon Law has always focused on the question of liceity (or licitness) instead, without which these actions are not done in the name of, nor recognized by, the Church — any potential theological validity is rendered moot. But Thục's defenders have sometimes argued that the Archbishop's freelance work was also licit, on the basis of a 'special mandate' issued to Thục by Pope Pius XI in 1938.[30] The document being referred to, far from being special, was typical of those given to newly-appointed legates in mission territories which, especially with the war in the Pacific already underway, could be cut off from regular communication at any time. The document grants "every necessary faculty … [for] purposes known unto us [the pope]."[31] It is a stretch beyond a stretch of the imagination that such faculties and purposes might have included creating bishops for cults and sects forty years later, completely contrary to Canon Law. The essence of *liceity* is to be in keeping with the spirit of the law, rather than just following the letter of the law which is the essence of *legality*. It is absurd to suggest that Thục may have been granted blanket permission to disregard Canon Law, which since 1951 expressly forbade bishops *of whatever rite or dignity* from consecrating without nomination or express confirmation by the Holy See, under pain of the highest level of excommunication.

It is impossible to say for certain what precise purposes Pius XI had in mind when appointing Thục as legate, but the granting of emergency wartime powers was par for the course. In effect, therefore, we are able to say what kind of purposes would *not* be intended; such powers were obviously not intended to be used in peacetime European countries with a stable hierarchy, when the bishop in question is without office and has been retired for a decade, when the legitimate Ordinary begs him not to proceed, and when there is no impediment to communicating with Rome on the issue (except unwillingness to do so). It is another example of needing to take account of the context and spirit of a text and not just the letter, in keeping with the basic principles and within the context of Canon Law. But what about the practical application of the Pius XI document; did Thục in practice have a free hand in consecrating whomsoever he pleased? Thục asserted to Guérard des Lauriers that as papal legate he had personally selected and consecrated all of Vietnam's bishops in the 1940's and 1950's,[32] but public record shows that this was simply not the case. It befell Thục to personally consecrate only two bishops in those years, and they were hardly his choices; Monsignor Hien, whose appointment Thục actually flew to Rome to try to block, and Monsignor Binh, who publicly rebuked Thục for his politicking and effectively banned him from the Saigon Archdiocese. It is fantasy to imagine that Thục at any point licitly consecrated bishops on his own initiative, without papal mandate.

Such hypothetical action could potentially have been considered legitimate in wartime, in the midst of battle, after the collapse of society, or in the case of the imprisonment en masse of the clergy, and Thục's legate powers were clearly designed for such catastrophic eventualities. In these cases, as with some consecrations in China or behind the Iron Curtain, the Holy See could retroactively mandate the appointment. But none of this ever happened to Thục; the Church in Vietnam did not cease to function either during the Japanese occupation or during the subsequent anti-colonial war. Sedevacantists could argue that the post-Vatican II Church really is in a state of emergency analogous to the catastrophe of wartime, that the collapse of decent godly society is no remote dystopia, and that there are no stable hierarchies or legitimate Ordinaries. But even if that were the case, it would not retroactively alter the spirit of the Thục document. Reading only the letter of the text and ignoring the spirit is a classic mistake of the theologically unversed, and also typical of the ancient heretics who "rigidly stuck to the letter in which no spirit dwelt."[33] It inevitably has to be pointed out that Thục himself surely knew all of this, and that he deliberately framed events to suggest that he had long been accustomed to operating freelance, with Church permission, innocently believing that he had every right to consecrate whomsoever he pleased. He was less than totally honest in the version of events given to Guérard des Lauriers, with respect to Thục's utterly fictitious non-mandated consecrations in Vietnam. The truth is that Thục had indeed always assumed the right to do as he pleased, especially back in his Vietnam days as part of the ruling junta, but it was not based on any papal documents or Canon Laws. Nor was it new for Thục to be intensely annoyed when he did not get away with it.

Looking beyond the documents, what really motivated Archbishop Thục? The significance of the year 1975 should not be underestimated. The Vietnam War reached its dramatic conclusion at the end of April. Thục's nephew had been named Auxiliary Bishop of Saigon just days before, and was now arrested as the sole representative of the Ngô regime, with the weight of his uncles' legacy on his shoulders. For Thục, the Vietnamese victory meant that he had definitively lost his property, his funds, and his right to return home. If he still held out a hope for those things, April 1975 put an end to that. As for his nephew in solitary confinement, there but for the grace of God went Thục. Indeed, Thục was the great survivor; three of his siblings had died in infancy, four of his brothers — Khôi, Diệm, Nhu, and Cân — were violently killed, along with countless former friends and parishioners in the intervening years, and two of Thục's nieces were killed in automobile accidents. In 1975 there was little talk of survivor's guilt syndrome and its varied and unpredictable effects. Survivor's guilt syndrome is now considered a significant symptom and aspect of Post-Traumatic Stress Disorder (PTSD), and must be seen as a probable factor in the Thục case which is not often mentioned.

The effects of PTSD vary according to the psychological profile of the sufferer, however, and Thục's prior behavior should raise concerns. All of the Ngôs believed themselves to be infallible and invulnerable; they demonstrated willful ignorance that their behavior might contradict the Christian values they claimed to uphold. Much like the stereotypically devout Catholic Mafia families, they believed that by definition they could do no wrong. The Ngô family culture was one of self-justification and self-righteousness, for example in Thục's blasé handling of sexual abuse and open accumulation of vast wealth. The Ngôs were internally united and self-sufficient, keeping outsiders outside and maintaining *omertà*-style secrecy. They had their own version of the Catholic religion, relativizing inconvenient tenets and precepts of their faith to accommodate and excuse their activities. Their tactics, like the Mob's, were violent repression, abduction and torture, fraud, insider trading, abuses of power, threats, misappropriation of goods, land, and cash, smuggling, drug use and drug dealing. Like *Capos*, they enjoyed the best clothes, cars and weapons (all thanks to the US purse). Thục shared their complexes, paranoia, megalomania, delusions and addiction to power; their feelings of omnipotence and superiority, belief in their own deceptions, and tendency to relativize the truth. Words like erratic and volatile were later used about Thục, but he had always been accustomed to doing whatever he wanted in order to get the job done; the flipsides of erratic and volatile may be creative and adaptable. He was, certainly, only human and fallible — power is described in terms of intoxication for good reason; it corrupts even good people. But in terms of evaluating Thục's psychological profile, for someone to be stripped of all that power and untouchability and to have their fragile mortality suddenly laid bare is bound to have terrible consequences for their mental health.

Four months after his final public appearance at the Marian Days, on 13th December 1984, Pierre Martin Ngô-dinh-Thục died of cancer at Carthage, Missouri, in the care of the CMC congregation.[34] He was at least able to end his days in an environment in which he could truly say that "everyone knows and respects the names Ngô-dinh-Diệm, father of the Republic of Vietnam, and Ngô-dinh-Nhu and Ngô-dinh-Cân, aides of the President."[35] Whatever acclaim Thục may have enjoyed at the end from the Vietnamese refugee community, only one remaining Ngô family member, his youngest brother Luyen, attended Thục's funeral. The formidable Madame Nhu did not attend. Luyen died in 1990, aged 76, and Madame Nhu died in 2011, aged 86. Thục's nephew, Bishop Nguyễn-van-Thuận, still imprisoned in Vietnam at the time of Thục's death, was released in 1988 and then exiled. He was made a cardinal by John Paul II in 2001 and died in 2002. The cause for Thuận's canonization took a step forward in 2017 when he was declared Venerable by the Vatican. Tuan Hoang, who was at the 1984 Marian Days with Thục, wrote that

"many of the Catholic refugees, especially members of the CMC, felt at least some closure and resolution about the last year of the Archbishop's life. ... it provided a small if not insignificant measure of solace to those refugees. In 1984, after all, they had no clear idea if they would ever see again their old churches, neighborhoods, the tombs of deceased family members, and of course loved ones still living. The 'return' of the Archbishop, I think, offered some of them a psychological boost to the long-standing belief in the righteousness of their Catholic practices."[36]

For the sedevacantist movement too, Thục provided a definite 'psychological boost to the long-standing belief in the righteousness of their Catholic practices.' His impact continues to be felt in the sedevacantist community, but so does the controversy: ironically, Thục's canonization as the 'grand old man' of sedevacantism has led to his posthumous demotion in the eyes of some members of the movement. Since they believe that John XXIII was in no position to appoint Thục as Archbishop of Huế, he remains, for some hardliners, plain old *Bishop* Thục as he was pre-1960.[37] There is also the ongoing controversy of the validity of the sacraments conferred: "Given the fact that Thục became the most prolific consecrator of traditionalists and other independent Catholics, the validity of his consecrations remains a constant matter of discussion in these circles,"[38] Magnus Lundberg observed. Thục himself, however, appears to had little time for such debates, as *Einsicht* recalled: "He was laconic; he could not stand long theologizing or pious talk";[39] nor was he inclined towards picking arguments; "hate and revenge were alien to him."[40] In any case, Archbishop Thục himself is above all such debates now. Even if sedevacantists, quasi-sedevacantists, and anti-sedevacantists are for the moment denied peace, may they all at least wish it upon Archbishop Thục — *resquiat in pace.*

Memor esto, Domine, opprobrii servorum tuorum:
quod continui in sinu meo, multarum gentium;
quod exprobraverunt inimici tui, Domine,
quod exprobraverunt commutationem christi tui.
Benedictus Dominus in æternum. Fiat! Fiat!

(Psalm 89)

(Remember, O Lord, how thy servant is scorned;
how I bear in my bosom the insults of the peoples;
with which thy enemies taunt, O Lord,
with which they mock the footsteps of thy anointed.
Blessed be the Lord forever. Amen! Amen!)

Notes

1   The title of Thục's autobiographical notes, written around 1976
2   James S. Olson and Randy Roberts, *Where the Domino Fell: America and Vietnam 1945 to 1990,* St. Martin's Press, New York, 1991, p 99
3   Ngô-dinh-Thục, 'Declaration,' *Einsicht,* Yr. 28, (Special Edition), April 1998 /2, Una Voce Group, Munich, pp 1-9 (translated from the Latin original on pp 1-4; the English and French translations provided by *Einsicht* are inaccurate).
4   Ngô-dinh-Thục, 'Misericordias Domini in Aeternum Cantabo: Autobiographie de Mgr. Pierre Martin Ngô-dinh-Thục, Archeveque de Huế' [sic], *Einsicht* (Special Edition), Una Voce-Gruppe Maria, Munich, August 1982, p 60
5   *New York Times,* 8th April 1983, p 5
6   Tuan Hoang, Pepperdine University, 'The Last Years of Ngô-dinh-Thục' – www.tuannyriver.com – https://tuannyriver.com/2017/08/21/the-last-years-of-ngo-dinh-thuc/ [accessed 10th June 2018]
7   *New York Times,* 10th June 1994, p 1
8   Tuan Hoang, op. cit.
9   Cf. Tuan Hoang, op. cit.
10 Diocese of Vinh Long, quoted and translated by Tuan Hoang, in 'The Last Years of Ngô-dinh-Thục' – https://tuannyriver.com/2017/08/21/the-last-years-of-ngo-dinh-thuc/ [accessed 10th June 2018]
11 *Einsicht,* Yr. 14, No. 6, February 1985, p 153
12 Tuan Hoang, op. cit.
13 Ibid.
14 Quoted in Charles Keith, *Catholic Vietnam: a Church from Empire to Nation,* 2012, p 177
15 Cf. Edward Jarvis, *God, Land & Freedom: The True Story of I.C.A.B.,* Apocryphile Press, Berkeley CA, 2018, pp 134-135
16 John P. Plummer, *The Many Paths of the Independent Sacramental Movement,* Apocryphile Press, Berkeley, CA, 2006, p 86
17 Peter Hebblethwaite, *The Runaway Church,* Collins Fount, Glasgow, 1978, p 246
18 Cf. (title of) Karl Prüter, *Bishops Extraordinary,* Saint Willibrord Press, Highlandville MO, 1985
19 David V. Barrett, *Sects, 'Cults' and Alternative Religions,* Blandford (a Cassell imprint), London, 1998 p 122
20 Cf. (title of) John P. Plummer and John R. Mabry, *Who Are The Independent Catholics?,* Apocryphile Press, Berkeley CA, 2006
21 Cf. John P. Plummer, op. cit. 2006 (title of)

22   Cf. John L. Allen Jr., *The Future Church,* Image, New York, 2009, p 91

23   See Edward Jarvis, op. cit.

24   Joseph Ratzinger, *Salt of the Earth,* Ignatius Press, San Francisco, 1997, p 16

25   Idem, p 222

26   Yves Congar, *Challenge to The Church – The Case of Archbishop Lefebvre,* Collins Liturgical Publications, London, 1977, p 72

27   Avery Dulles, *The Catholicity of the Church,* Clarendon Press, Oxford, 1987, p 66

28   Cf. Magnus Lundberg, *A Pope of their Own: El Palmar de Troya and the Palmarian Church,* Uppsala Studies in Church History 1, Uppsala University, Department of Theology, 2017, p 75

29   Clarence Kelly, *The Sacred and the Profane,* Seminary Press, Round Top NY, 1997, p 12

30   Cf. Fraternité Notre Dame, http://www.fraternitenotredame. com/2011_2_0/succession.php [accessed 16th June 2018] — *nb.* their translation from Latin is inaccurate.

31   *Einsicht,* Yr. 28, (Special Edition), April 1998 /2, Una Voce Group, Munich, p 13

32   Cf. Guérard des Lauriers, interview, *Sodalitium,* No. 13, March 1988, (French) pp 18-34, and (Spanish) [pp 2-17], p 10

33   Johann Adam Möhler, *Unity in the Church or the Principle of Catholicism,* Catholic University of America Press, Washington DC, 1996, pp 141-142

34   Cf. Spencer C. Tucker (ed), *The Encyclopedia of the Vietnam War, a Political, Social, and Military History,* ABC-CLIO, Santa Barbara CA, 2011, p 813

35   Ngô-dinh-Thục, op. cit. 1982, p 13

36   Tuan Hoang, op. cit.

37   See Mario Derksen, *'An Open Letter to Bishop Clarence Kelly on the "Thục Bishops" and the errors in* The Sacred and the Profane,*'* Cincinnati OH, 8th January 2011, www.thucbishops.com [accessed 6th June 2018]

38   Magnus Lundberg, op. cit. 2017, p 75

39   *Einsicht,* Yr. 14, No. 6, February 1985, p 153

40   Ibid.

VIII

OCTAVUM CAPITULUM

— THEOLOGICAL QUESTIONS ARISING FROM THE THỤC CASE —

When westerners contemplate Christianity in Asia, they typically expect the most striking differences to be the external features. They may expect elements such as worship style, music, dress, greetings, etc. to display distinctive local characteristics, assuming that the basic ideas and philosophical concepts underpinning the Christian religion are bound to be fundamentally the same everywhere; otherwise, it would be difficult to call it the same religion. In reality, the reverse is more likely to be true: maintaining a uniform external appearance, especially with detailed and approved liturgical books to follow, can be much easier than adapting to and assimilating an alien social, cultural, and philosophical mindset. Christianity, arguably a Western religion with its own social and cultural concepts and language, did not arrive in Asia to find a blank slate; it encountered a range of ancient, pre-existing, and deep-rooted social and cultural concepts and language. Over time, proponents of Christianity started to accept that it was utterly hopeless to try to uproot the local philosophies and religions, because even with the roots gone, the very soil of Asia was steeped in local ways and worldviews.[1]

This was the world of the Ngôs. The Catholicism they experienced was a localized form and expression of it, sitting in harmony with other well-established local beliefs and customs.[2] This prospect is neither blasphemous nor unusual in Southeast Asia, where elements of more than one religion may be believed in conjunction with one another, especially when there is no explicit contradiction — the Christian scriptures do not address reincarnation, for example. The Ngô brothers themselves, reflecting on their upbringing, described it as "Confucian and Catholic."[3] Surely, there will also have been elements of the European missionaries' approach, their attitudes and values, which were less than edifying and which local converts wanted to reject. Just as the Christian scriptures do not expressly rule out reincarnation or ancestor worship, there is no explicit support for colonialism or condemnation of national liberation. As a priest and then bishop, Thục strongly backed the development of a patriotic, native clergy, and encouraged the departure of the European missionaries.[4] He defended local interpretations of Catholicism and complained about the Church's tendency toward "the leveling of all particularities inherent in every civilization — which, by the way, is the work of the good God, who takes pleasure in Unity and also in Diversity."[5]

> "The Vatican invents regulations to quash whatever peculiarity, whether liturgical or canonical, of the 'lesser' Churches. It wants uniformity everywhere, without thinking that each people possesses its own characteristics just as respectable as those of Rome. Here are some examples: for the Roman, as a sign of respect, one stands up; in Vietnam, we kneel. The Roman extends his arms in prayer; the Vietnamese clasps his hands together to pray. Europeans shake hands as a sign of friendship or by way of greeting; Asians, Chinese, Vietnamese, put their hands together and bow their head, and the bow will be deeper according to the respectability of the one we are greeting."[6]

Thục called diversity "the ornament of the Universe. Why impose a single way of celebrating Holy Mass — which consists solely of the Consecration — and to impose this under pain of suspension and even excommunication; is this not the abuse of power?"[7] Thục proudly admitted that this was his independent Vietnamese spirit talking, his Vietnamese patriotism. The Ngôs, though Catholic,

138

were still "Việt through and through. From a Christian perspective, we are obedient to the Roman Church … we accept unanimity in dogmas of faith, but alongside diversity in areas that do not concern dogma."[8]

By the 1970's theologians were talking of 'third world theology' in addition to 'liberation theology.' But as we have seen previously, 'third' world was not to be understood primarily in the sense of ranking or position, after the capitalist 'free world' and the communist bloc, but more in keeping with the original French usage of *tiers monde*. The idea of *tiers monde* connotes an *alternative world* to be aspired to – a third way. These distinctions are important for understanding the mindset of Archbishop Thục, because this is precisely the model of the future that people in nations such as Vietnam looked towards, having experienced one of the other ways — colonial domination — and rejecting the other — economic imperialism. The third way meant exploring a form in which to be truly self-determining. The decolonized nations of the 1950's and 1960's, whether in Africa, Asia, or the Mediterranean, aimed to resist the threat of becoming mere satellites of one world bloc or the other — colonialism by another name. The Non-Aligned Movement became the most salient organized political expression of this new awareness. This sense of 'third world' as *tiers monde* also corresponds to the Greek Fathers of the Church when they applied the same word *triton (genos)* to Christianity. This was in order to emphasize that their religion was neither a Judaic nor a Hellenistic religion, but a *tertium quid,* a 'third something.'[9] In the light of this understanding, a Vietnamese Catholic like Thục need have had no difficulty reconciling the Christian and Southeast Asian worldviews, looking beyond any apparently conflicting elements to find a harmonious third way.

Though the term 'third world' need not be seen in a negative light, it is evident that for multiple historical reasons the third world has indeed been left in third place in many senses — it has been distinguished both by its mass poverty and for its being exploited by the other two worlds. The third world is also, however, numerically superior, including in numbers of Christians, which has prompted some to refer to it as the 'two-thirds world.'[10] In the middle decades of the twentieth century the Asian third world started to show its potential might. Vietnam, for example, resoundingly defeated two world powers: first France and then America. China's unaided rise to the level of economic, political, and military superpower also gave a boost to Asian consciousness. Liberation theology began to put down roots in Asia, as Asians started to reject the idea of 'being developed' from without, seeing the big world powers as centers of domination rather than development. But it also took on characteristics of its own; Asian liberation theology has been less driven by an affinity to Marxism than its counterpart in Latin America. Even so, the aversion to unbridled capitalism (or Mammon-worship) professed by socialist governments led to greater sympathy for the communist worldview than for the transatlantic one.[11]

The origins of Asian liberationism and Thục's own thought system are closely related: he too was unapologetically mistrustful with regard to the 'dominant' nations; he found his own recipe to combine traditional Southeast Asian and European Christian values;[12] he was opposed to "the leveling of all particularities inherent in every civilization."[13] The Ngô brand of Catholicism was, Thục admitted, a "combative Catholicism,"[14] which strove for independence, diversity, and reserved the right to express itself. The later Asian liberationists would build on this kind of quasi-nationalistic thinking: "Christ does not compete with the founders of other religions but cross-fertilizes Asian religiosity [and] Christianity does not compete with other religions but complements them."[15]

> "The result is neither "syncretism" (a cocktail of religions in which the specific flavor of each religion is modified by that of the others) nor "synthesis" (creation of something entirely new out of the component religions which have, in the process, lost their separate identities altogether), but a *symbiosis* of religions."[16]

These are broadly the principles of Asian-nuanced Christianity and Catholicism. They are deeply inculcated bases of understanding, which predated Thục and which permeated his worldview and faith. In light of this it is easy to see how Thục easily sailed with the tide of Vatican II thinking.

The standard post-Vatican II view that "variety is a sign of richness — not a mistake, failure, or weakness"[17] strikes a clear chord with Thục's theology. But he seemed to fight himself into a corner when he complained that only the old Mass of Pius V was outlawed by the post-Vatican II Church. Thục appeared to be defending the continued use of the old Mass more on a principle of allowing diversity, rather than for theological reasons and the defense of tradition. In his defense, post-Vatican II thinking on diversity can seem inconsistent, especially when there was a perceived danger of revolt from this or that wing of the Church. The threat of schism can send even committed liberals retreating into reactionary shells; Yves Congar described a schismatic as "someone who wants to think, pray, act — in a word, live — not in harmony with the whole Church ... but according to his own rules and like an autonomous being."[18] Not a very valiant stand for diversity and individuality from Cardinal Congar. Is the schismatic really the one 'who wants to think, pray, act like an autonomous being'? Are orthodox thought, prayer, and action all equally essential, and in the same way?

Approaches to keeping a shared faith have often tended to focus on essentials, which St. Vincent of Lerins described as that which has been believed in the Church "*quod ubique, quod semper, quod ab omnibus*" — everywhere, always, by everyone.[19] Thục may have been basically correct when he observed that the pre-Vatican II Church had had a clearer idea of what the essentials were, while accommodating a certain and perhaps unavoidable degree of diversity. His own inconsistency could simply be symptomatic of the Church's general inability to reconcile unity and diversity. The failure to clearly identify what the essentials are leads to fuzziness, but aiming to stamp out everything but the bare essentials has dangers too. Traditionalist Catholicism can be regimented and stifling in a way that the old Church was not. The current trend is to quote papal bulls and theological treatises at the slightest prompting, firing off chapter, verse, and page numbers like the most fundamentalist Pentecostals, lest any suspect comment or dangerous doubt sneak through the barrage of citations. Every strictly policed thought must be backed up with names and quotes from the traditionalist canon, echoing the ancient heretics who "rigidly stuck to the letter in which no spirit dwelt,"[20] as Johann Adam Möhler wrote. For Möhler, lack of diversity was actually a feature of heresy, since "true Christian life is not possible in any heresy because there are no antitheses in heresy."[21]

Thục's most theologically controversial actions were his unauthorized episcopal consecrations. He asked in his memoir, "Would a certain Paul of Tarsus have been, nowadays, excommunicated by a certain Peter, because he consecrated bishops without referring to Peter?"[22] But Thục knew of course that the early Church, in order to expand and survive, had quite reasonably developed rules and guidelines since the days of Peter and Paul. In the first centuries, the Church was quite aware that some bishops arrogated the right to consecrate freely — or freelance — without assigning a proper jurisdiction, and not always with the right motivations and selection criteria. Councils of the Church, particularly Chalcedon (451), expressly and vehemently forbade this. Even in 451, the Church was no fool, and it was clear then as it is now that randomly distributed Holy Orders could open the door to corruption, deception, and misbehavior; Palmar de Troya and some of Thục's other ill-advised connections provide abundant proof. It is of course absolutely necessary to point out that among the family tree of Thục's bishops there are also examples of the noblest and most dignified of motivations. But this does not change the general truth that the unfettered and unchecked consecration of bishops over the years — whether via Duarte Costa, Emmanuel Milingo, or Ngô-dinh-Thục — has tended to be bad news both for the individuals and for the Church. This subject merits some attention because it has become such a distinguishing feature of both the sedevacantist movement and the broader Independent Catholic movement.

The freelance or autonomous consecration of new bishops has the potential to go from being an emergency measure to an institutional characteristic of the sedevacantist movement; Thục's original behavior has in fact become fossilized in the movement he backed. This is, ironically, a major departure from the practice of the Church. Whatever the possible flaws or faults in the Church's procedure for selecting bishops (and it has been much criticized over the centuries), a significant number of people are at least involved in the selection process. But consider these recent words of sedevacantist Bishop Sanborn, announcing the appointment of a new bishop: "Obviously sooner or later I had to choose someone to succeed me in what I do and say [sic]. I will be sixty-eight in February. I have been mulling over doing this consecration for quite a while."[23] It is all too clear how few people were involved in this particular selection, what factors prompted the supposed need for a new bishop, and also what the main criteria were. There is scant precedent in the Church for a bishop unilaterally 'mulling' over whom to appoint as their personal successor, with a mandate to perpetuate what they 'do and say.' This is the reality of the sedevacantist movement.

In terms of the actual choosing of a successor, Sanborn claimed to have chosen "the obvious candidate to be a bishop. He has been under my tutelage continually since he was six years old. He is thoroughly familiar with all of our principles and ways of acting."[24] Sanborn assumed the roles of diocese, episcopal conference, congregation for bishops, and Holy See; but when such an 'obvious candidate' is right in front of you, why not? After all, only the consecrating bishop needs to be convinced. "I have not yet set a date for the consecration, since to be a bishop requires a great deal of preparation from the point of view of robes and other paraphernalia."[25] Unfortunately the priorities in play here are extremely clear, and they have little to do with the traditional practice of the Church. Of course, the defense would be, and will always be, that there is a crisis in the Church and there is a need to act: but this is the same logic that has so far crowned a dozen sedevacantist 'popes,' including David Bawden — who was elected by six people, including himself and his parents.

Freelance consecration is a trend that seems to lead to a great deal of self-importance and self-deception, but this is by no means restricted to the world of the Thục bishops. Consider the case of 'Married Priests Now!' (MPN), the rebel group founded by Archbishop Milingo. In 2006 Milingo famously consecrated four married men, who had all been previously consecrated (up to four times) as 'Duarte Costa' bishops or 'Old Catholic' bishops. "Our present intention," they announced, "is to mesh with the institutional church and our only goal is to have married priests honored and returned to full ministry and to have married men ordained to the priesthood."[26] This approach showed little understanding of the workings of the Church, though the men in question must have had a collective experience of about 100 years dealing with Rome. It is almost as if receiving multiple consecrations somehow cuts the rope anchoring an individual to reality. Why did the 'Married Priests Now!' cohort feel that their case could only be served by becoming unauthorized, unrecognized, freelance bishops? Here is their answer:

> "The institutional church understands hierarchy and respects the office of bishop. Our prelature retains the hierarchical structure (with mitres) [sic] because it allows the institutional church to rec-ognize us as Catholic and Episcopal; and is a sign that we mean business. They are comfortable with that structure and know what it means."[27]

These statements must unfortunately be called out as delusional, and for them to have come from four men with advanced theological degrees and years of study is surprising. It does not take a canny Vatican insider to know that the Church is unlikely to be persuaded to change its centuries-old rules because the people requesting it have made the effort to wear miters. Barely a word of the statement could ever be acceptable to the Vatican: the four men in question are not 'hierarchy' and have no 'office'; it is not a 'prelature' and cannot be regarded as a 'structure,' 'Catholic,' or 'Episcopal' in the senses that the Vatican uses these terms. The MPN approach is not a convincing display of theological, ecclesiological, and canonical savoir faire. Thục too, it will be recalled, had studied at some of the best universities and allegedly had three pontifical doctorates, as well as years of pastoral experience in the Church. It is not unreasonable to wonder how he could be taken in by the Palmar pantomime, or how he could have agreed to just consecrate whoever the 'generous Germans' brought to his bedroom. But whatever short-circuited inside Thục's head, his is not an isolated case. In practically all the cases of unauthorized episcopal consecrations over the last 100 years, the consecrating bishops involved have drifted into imprudent and reckless endeavors. In exercising their powers they have generally ended up either abusing their powers, ordaining seriously troubled individuals, or in some cases, dispensing sacraments in return for favors, attention, and money. They have often deceived and often been deceived; Bishop Arnold Harris Mathew was even deceived into believing that an entire 'British Old Catholic Church' had elected him bishop — it did not exist. Once again, whatever may be said against Thục, he was not alone. Sedevacantists would rather not see themselves as part of the 'Independent Catholic' movement at all, but there are clear interrelationships and similarities of praxis which mean that the phenomena must be considered side by side.

It is evident from the outside that the main motivation in the Independent Catholic world is to break the current Vatican's apparent monopoly on Catholicism and to challenge its supposed right to dictate what is and what is not Catholic identity. Even sedevacantism can be seen as a variation on this, challenging the Vatican's legitimacy in a particular way. From the inside, groups such as MPN and various other freelance or independent bishops generally insist, as Thục did, that their goal is to save the Church.

A wide range of Independent Catholic groups, both progressive and traditionalist, appeal to the principle of *lex suprema salus animarum* — the supreme law of the Church is the salvation of souls — by way of justification. It is a favorite all-embracing get-out clause of renegades and rebels. Karl Rahner cited the *lex suprema* in the context of justifying the ordination of married men and women.[28] The *lex suprema* forms part of Canon 1752 of the (current) Code of Canon Law. Canon 1752 is the last of the canons, and makes *reference* — this point is crucial — to the *lex suprema*. It does not appear in the Code as a stand-alone law, and the whole canon reads as follows:

> "In cases of transfer [of pastors] the prescripts of can. 1747 are to be applied, canonical equity is to be observed, and the salvation of souls, which must always be the supreme law of the Church, is to be kept before one's eyes."

While the supreme law, as Thomas J. Paprocki wrote, "helps make the law approachable" for the uninitiated, it must not "lose its effectiveness ... by becoming too easily invoked in any and every situation."[29] The danger with such an all-embracing maxim is obvious: it "could be cited for conflicting sides of the same argument. ... Each could argue his position based on his concern for the supreme law of the Church."[30] To reach agreement would require reference to other canons, providing those appealing to the supreme law are not under the illusion that its invocation renders the rest of the Code of Canon Law irrelevant. Canon 1752 *refers* to the 'supreme law' — it is not 'the supreme canon' that trumps all the others, and nor was it a canon in the 1917 Code. The supreme law 'is to be kept before one's eyes' in harmony with the rest of the canons, and "that is only one reason why the Code of Canon Law contains one thousand seven hundred and fifty-two canons instead of just this one supreme law!"[31] The whole of the law – and every canon – in fact must be directed towards the salvation of souls, as an expression of the whole collective effort of the Church.

A typical appeal to the supreme law would state that the consecrating bishop is providing priests, and therefore providing access to the sacraments, for a group of faithful who for some reason have been isolated from the regular hierarchy. But this argument may betray a superficial or inadequate understanding of what the salvation of souls is, equating salvation with frequent access to the sacraments by any means. Furthermore, it promotes an image of the priest as intermediary and savior, the dispenser of sacraments; salvation depends on having access to *him* rather than on being in communion with the Church, and this risks distorting Catholic theology. When a group perceives itself as 'saving the Church' or 'revitalizing the Church' or 'returning the Church to tradition,' it echoes, according to Johann Adam Möhler, the attitude of the ancient heretics, for whom "the preservation of Christian doctrine must be viewed as a human work because they believed that *they* were to call upon human beings to discover it again."[32] This conviction stems from a basic lack of faith in the "Holy Spirit who continually preserves the Church, [which is] formed and enlivened by that Spirit,"[33] and not by human saviors, Möhler explained. The heretic believes in human saviors coming to the rescue, not God. Enlightened groups of Church-savers, whether progressive or traditionalist, tend to break away from mainstream parishes as though "Christianity and Christ could be grasped most certainly in a separatistic and egotistic manner aside from any Church community."[34] This is echoed in Richard McBrien's observation that the opposite of Catholic is Sectarian rather than Protestant, as is often thought.[35] For heretics, the faith is constantly slipping from our grasp, and it is always a good time for drastic action. All of this unfortunately rings very true of traditionalist and sedevacantist movements, who long to see ordinary Catholicism purged of all its flaws, and for their pure version to receive universal recognition.

So what about the flaws in sedevacantist thinking, in the eyes of ordinary Catholics? Sedevacantism holds that the recent popes were not true popes because of heresy — but does the one elected pope not at least have a say in what constitutes heresy? The key Vatican II heresy would be Modernism, but was Modernism actually declared a heresy? Were its adherents all duly excommunicated, as heretics would be? And what about the chair being literally vacant — *sede vacante* — since the current church in Rome does have a properly elected leader? Is the pope something other than leader of the church in Rome then? At what stage in the historical development of the Papacy did the pope acquire this other nature? Bishop Guérard des Lauriers, consecrated by Thục in 1981, proposed a complex thesis which distinguished the *material* nature of the Papacy (being the properly elected leader of the Roman church) from its *formal* nature (being spiritually Christ's vicar on earth). John Paul II, he said, was pope in the first, administrative, sense but not the second, spiritual sense. Guérard des Lauriers' chosen course of action — to be consecrated bishop by Thục — contradicts his theory, however, because he responds to an administratively legitimate pope with administratively disobedient actions (schism), even though that same legitimate administration might well provide a fully 'material *and* formal' pope in the future. Archbishop Marcel Lefebvre used the terms Catholic Rome and Eternal Rome to distinguish this spiritual, ethereal Rome from the de facto administrative reality of the actual church in Rome:

> "We adhere with all our heart and all our soul to Catholic Rome, guardian of the Catholic faith and the traditions necessary to maintain it, and to Eternal Rome, mistress of wisdom and truth.
>
> On the other hand we refuse and have always refused to follow the Rome of the neo-Modernist and the new Protestant trend which was clearly evident in the Second Vatican Council and, after the Council, in all the reforms which flowed from it."[36]

But one searches in vain for the historical and theological precedents for this ideological division — the real Rome with a bricks and mortar church and a theology that we do not like vs. a quasi-mythological Eternal, Catholic Rome full of saints. The primacy of Rome, as is well known, took some time to emerge historically;

one wonders then, where this idealized 'Eternal Rome' was during the first centuries of the Church.

It is perhaps ironic that in these recent decades which have seen the Papacy challenged and disputed more than ever before, people have truly loved the popes.[37] At a personal level they have generally been 'peacefully accepted' as popes, in the phrase of the Jesuit theologian Louis Billot.[38] Debating the nature and role of the Papacy, however, is no longer taboo: "For the first time it is the Pope himself who raises and legitimizes the question of reform and change in the papal office in the Church."[39] Nor is the push to reform the Papacy necessarily aimed at the pope: "It is not the authority of the pope which is in doubt among faithful sons of the Church, but the 'system' which holds him prisoner."[40] Some features of this papal 'system,' certain sons of the Church believe, obviously once served a purpose but may need reforming or indeed abolishing — bureaucracy, secrecy, curial careerism and nefarious activities. Even, or perhaps especially, within mainstream Catholicism, the Papacy is no longer untouchable or above criticism. Referring to the 'validity' of the pope is problematic, because validity is a term properly applied to the sacraments, and this encourages the notion that papal enthronement is a kind of sacrament, which it is not. The spread of this notion could be useful to the sedevacantist case, however, keeping the Papacy in the realm of mystery rather than administration, and in fact, the Palmarian Church did declare Papacy as the eighth sacrament. The papal vacancy has a special place in sedevacantist thinking as the symbol of everything wrong in the Church, while it is also institutionally fundamental because it absolves the movement from identifying a high-point of authority that would be able to condemn what they do. The crisis in the Church means that all the norms of practice and procedure are suspended — crisis itself may be one of sedevacantism's chief attractions.

Traditionalist *non*-sedevacantist Catholics expend great energy, understandably, in trying to silence or eliminate their extreme cousins the sedevacantists, and with good reason. But it is disingenuous not to admit that the sedevacantists have a point. Both pre- and post-Vatican II Catholic theology hold that the Catholic faithful's acceptance and reception, both of a pope and his teaching, are a surefire sign of the pope's legitimacy. The Church, after all, is infallible too, though this infallibility is less famous than papal infallibility. The Church, Catholic theology holds, would be incapable of adhering to and obeying a false pope. The salient problem for the anti-sedevacantists is this: who could say that the last fifty years in Catholicism have been characterized by the wholesale acceptance or reception of Church teaching, considering *Humanae Vitae*, the reality of the declining Catholic family, the dearth of vocations, and the stealthy legalization of abortion in Catholic-majority countries? Who would describe these decades of catholic revolt, protest, and schism — both progressive and traditionalist — as times of general adherence and obedience to the popes? Catholicism has never experienced anything quite like it, though it is important to point out that dissent is expressed more easily and freely than before. There are a multitude of social, legal, technological and spiritual reasons for this. Dissent is also more easily — in fact, instantly — communicable. We do not therefore have the tools to measure dissent in the Church of sixty years ago and more, though by their actions Catholics certainly demonstrated a different level of acceptance of the popes and reception of their teaching, compared to today. The diminishing size of the Catholic family alone since the pill, or since 1968, speaks volumes. In Italy, Spain, Portugal, Ireland, Argentina, etc. the Catholic birth rate has been almost literally decimated.

We cannot know for certain how the accessibility of contraception would have impacted the Catholic world had it appeared in 1908 instead of 1968, but the outcome for the anti- and pro-sedevacantist debate is not actually affected. The point is that today's situation is clearly characterized by a new tradition in which Church teaching is habitually resisted or dismissed outright; it is absolutely routine to at worst ridicule and at best quietly reject the pope's statements. Actually adhering to the current pope and assimilating his teaching, in the senses that a St. Pius X or a Pius XII would have expected as a bare minimum, would have to consist of more than simply acknowledging that Francis is really, truly pope — it is necessary for Catholics to put their allegiance where their mouth is. And the question of Vatican II is a real sticking point — nobody can deny that change in the Church has been sweeping and profound. Asking whether what results is in fact the same religion, in theory and practice, as before Vatican II is not moot, and the possible answers have contingencies and implications. Plenty of modern, liberal Catholics would agree without difficulty that today's Catholicism is not the same religion as a hundred years ago. Change has always been a feature of the Church, of course — it could be argued that the reforms were inevitably radical because the Church had been unnaturally static and rigid during the preceding decades, in order to survive the threats of wars, dictatorships, and revolutions.

The weighty task of the sedevacantists is to make stick a charge of heresy against the people expressly responsible for defining heresy — the pope, the cardinals, the bishops, and the theologians. The term perhaps most frequently used in traditionalist criticism of Vatican II and its reforms is Modernism. Modernism in the Catholic sense arose in the late nineteenth century as a loose movement of theologians and other scholars. Modernists challenged the established schools of scholarship, applying modern methods of analysis to scripture and moral theology, for example. Modernism was influenced by both Protestant and secular thought and tended to lead towards liberal theological conclusions. Modernism was largely the precursor of what has evolved into mainstream, modern Catholic scholarship and practice, so much so that referring to the 'Modernist movement' has become obsolete; nowadays the term Modernist is likely to only be used in a deprecating way, by the modern Church's detractors such as sedevacantists. All this is broadly undisputed. Mainstream Catholic theologians would, generally speaking, say that elements of the Modernist approach, which was revolutionary at its beginning, have been harmoniously integrated into modern theology, though not before time and debate removed Modernism's sharper edges and limited its possible excesses.

For sedevacantists, this general acceptance and admission of Modernism are proof positive of the modern Church's heresy, working from the top down. The most potent source for this claim is Pope St. Pius X's encyclical letter *Pascendi Dominici Gregis* of 1907, in which he calls Modernism (in part 39) 'the synthesis of all heresies.' But this statement is problematic, not straightforward. There is no doubt that Pius X strenuously and repeatedly denounced Modernism; he condemned and proscribed its key features one by one. There was no greater earthly evil facing the Church in his opinion, and his fight against it characterized his pontificate. But Pius X did not declare Modernism a heresy, and he did not itemize the specific *heresies* which Modernism is supposed to synthesize. To condemn and proscribe something is one thing, but to declare something a heresy is another — there can be no 'Well, obviously what he meant to say was...' when reading papal documents. Nor did he actually define his phrase 'the synthesis of all heresies.' This is problematic because there have been countless heresies in the course of two thousand years which Modernism clearly did not promote or even mention; 'all heresies' would, if meant literally, include the 'classic' heresies of Apollinarism, Docetism, Iconoclasm, Montanism, which were all formally declared heresies, while Modernism never was. It would be sensationalist to suggest that Modernism was so boundless that it could have led to all those bizarre and long-since resolved heresies of early Christianity — and, in fact, it did not lead to them; Modernism was toned-down and held to account and reason.

The phrase 'synthesis of all heresies' is without precedent or identifiable prior usage, making it difficult to make comparisons and get to the core of what Pius X meant. Could he have meant it literally? In the sense of Modernism comprising all previous heresies, no, but in the sense of it being a method of scholarship so dangerously open-ended that any conclusion is possible, yes. He was not making a charge of heresy against Modernists but explaining that their approach opened the door to heresy. This is evident from *Pascendi Dominici Gregis* itself, in which Pius X describes at length the spread of Modernism, but at no point suggests that any of those involved are excommunicated. He calls for greater censorship, for gatherings of priests to be restricted, and for Modernists to be prevented from publishing. He does not call them out as heretics or suggest that they are outside the Church, or suspended, or have lost office (if priests or bishops). What was stopping him? Undoubtedly, whatever Modernism meant to Pius X, he did not explicitly declare it a heresy. But did he imply it? No, because while Pius X exhorted the Church to curtail the activities of Modernist priests — impede them from publishing books and holding meetings — it would have taken fewer words to point out that they were simply excommunicated, with all that that entails. The canonical crime of heresy would incur automatic excommunication, not requiring a pronouncement, but it would then be utterly superfluous to declare that excommunicated priests could not hold meetings or publish books in the Church's name. The opposite implication is therefore clear, that the Modernists were not excommunicated per se, and had not lost whatever offices they held, because if Modernism is not a heresy, Modernists cannot be guilty of the heresy of Modernism. This does not mean of course that some individual Modernists were not excommunicated on the basis of their individual actions, and not necessarily for heresy.

Thục, as we know, was excommunicated at least twice (that is, twice publicly) but even an excommunicated bishop can confer valid sacraments. What is meant by 'valid' and 'invalid' in the case of sacraments? These are deceptively commonplace words and their everyday uses do not correspond to their theological uses. 'Valid' may mean official, or legally and morally right; in the case of a passport or ticket it means that it is current and recognized; valid can also simply mean reasonable or good. These meanings are only coincidentally similar to theological sacramental validity. The sacraments are understood as efficacious signs of God's grace enacted through His Church; in practical terms they are rites of passage and investitures of sacred roles. They are milestones of a person's faith life – Baptism, Confirmation, Matrimony, the Last Rites. Two of the sacraments, the Eucharist (or Holy Communion) and Confession are particular in that they are meant to be repeated throughout life – repeating any of the other five sacraments is considered sacrilege. Validity means that these sacraments are administered to full effect and actually transmit God's graces. Can a Catholic really know that the sacrament has 'worked'? There is a sort of guarantee. In Catholic theology, the validity of the sacraments is assured because the minister has, in turn, been made a minister validly — he has validly received the sacrament of Holy Orders.

The chain must be demonstrably unbroken — a bishop ordains priests, some of whom are later consecrated bishop, and they go on to ordain more priests, who in turn provide the sacraments to the people. This 'genealogy' of ministers traces back through a vast family tree of bishops who succeeded bishops, in theory leading back to one or other of the Apostles — it is therefore referred to as the Apostolic Succession. In practice, detailed records of this 'family tree' are usually only reliable back to the sixteenth or seventeenth century. Once Apostolic Succession is established there are then only three criteria for the conferral of a valid sacrament: the correct *Matter* – things, actions, and people involved in the ceremony; the correct *Intention* – to do what the Church usually does when conferring the sacrament, for example intending to make a new priest; and the correct *Form* – the essential *words* of the rite. In order to challenge the validity of a sacrament, or for there to be a doubt over the validity, one of these three criteria would have to be 'defective.' Other flaws may be considered wrong or sacrilegious, such as the repeated or multiple reception of Holy Orders, or conferring some sacraments outside of Mass, or even the minister being a heretic, apostate, or schismatic, without necessarily affecting the validity.

The ordaining minister is traditionally *presumed* to have the correct sacramental *Intention* as long as the correct sacramental

Form — the Roman Pontifical — has been employed. Canon Law never presumes to know what is going on inside a person. Consequently it would be difficult to make a pronouncement about a minister's sacramental intention. Logically, the use of the *Form* prescribed by the Church is the most clear and obvious indicator that the ordaining bishop also has the correct *Intention* prescribed by the Church. Pope Pius XII's 1947 encyclical letter *Sacramentum Ordinis* set out the minimum essential line of text that must constitute the form of the sacrament of Holy Order. There have always been rumors that Thuc's consecration ceremonies, both in 1976 and 1981, were full of omissions, mistakes, or even celebrated outside of Mass (in Palmar de Troya). Even if this were so, the likelihood that he would have omitted — or agreed to omit, or been allowed to omit — the essential one line of text to validate the sacrament seems slim. In any case Canon Law is generous and reasonable where it might be expected to be unforgiving and strict — it is also often simple when it might be expected to be complex. 'What the Church does' in an ordination is make a new priest. If the ordaining minister understands even in general and unsophisticated terms what a priest is, then they can intend to make one. Whether they lean towards a traditional or modern theology of the priesthood, whether their understanding of priesthood is profound or shallow, or even if they hope to receive money or accommodation for ordaining said priest, these are all irrelevant where validity is concerned.

The Archdiocese of Acapulco adhered to a less generous interpretation of Canon Law when it reported in a "Warning to Priests"[41] that Sebastiano Cardinal Baggio, the Prefect of the Vatican Congregation for Bishops, had publicly stated that the consecrations of Carmona and Zamora were invalid, "because the ordaining minister *'non est compos sui.'*"[42] This is not to be confused with that other Latin phrase *non est compos mentis* — does not have control of his mind; whereas the phrase used here means that he does not have control of himself, or of his actions. The Vatican usually errs on the side of caution rather than declare ordinations and consecrations invalid, preferring to say that it does not recognize and will not recognize such ordinations. In practice this places technical, theological validity in second place to recognition — licitness, or liceity.

Valid or not, conferring the sacrament of Holy Orders is not designed to spring from the individual initiative of the minister, but to be a response to a call arising from the Church community.[43] The Council of Chalcedon (451) condemned consecrations that were not grounded in such a call, and 'freelance' consecrations were always regarded as null and void.[44] Such bishops were reminded that their power was in origin delegated power which should be rooted in a community. The more recklessly and arbitrarily a bishop exercises his power to ordain, for example, the more he deviates from the will and tradition of the Church, his mandate. It may become impossible to presume that his intention is the same as the Church's — ordaining a priest must simply mean something else to him. This is demonstrated in the case of Archbishop Milingo, who was excommunicated in 2006 after consecrating the four married men as bishops. He was laicized in 2009 and the Vatican stated that any further ordinations by Milingo the layman would be invalid as well as unrecognized.[45]

Even though it is open to being abused, Apostolic Succession is hailed in Western Catholicism as a guarantee of continuity and stability, while Eastern Orthodoxy takes the opposite view — the validity of Holy Orders stems from the stability of the Church which gives its mandate. "This view insists that valid orders depend upon the Church's life, and that authorization by the whole Church is an integral part of their validity."[46] In practice though, the Roman Catholic Church enforces the same policy as the Orthodox. Rome does not recognize and will not recognize Duarte Costa's, Milingo's, or Thục's ordinations and consecrations, absolutely and utterly regardless of whether or not they are technically valid. Theological validity has no currency without the Church's endorsement, as Canon VI of the Council of Chalcedon asserted, and it has never been up to freelance bishops to change that, irrespective of Vatican II. The perpetuation of the Thục 'line' only seems to lead to repeating his mistakes. Whatever the validity or invalidity, the merits or demerits of Thục's actions, his legacy will not be the salvation of the Roman Catholic Church as these words are usually understood at present. How people's understanding of these three words might evolve remains to be seen; how exactly they were understood by Archbishop Thục we will never really know.

Notes

[1]   Cf. Aloysius Pieris, 'Political Theologies in Asia,' Ch 18 in Peter Scott and William T. Cavanaugh (Eds),
        The Blackwell Companion to Political Theology, Blackwell, Oxford, 2004, [pp 256-270], p 259

[2]   Cf. idem, pp 259-260

[3]   James S. Olson and Randy Roberts, *Where the Domino Fell: America and Vietnam 1945 to 1990,* St. Martin's Press, New York, 1991, p 55

[4]   Cf. Charles Keith, *Catholic Vietnam: a Church from Empire to Nation,* University of California Press, Berkeley CA, 2012, p 177

[5]   Ngô-dinh-Thục, *'Misericordias Domini in Aeternum Cantabo': Autobiographie de Mgr. Pierre Martin Ngô-dinh-Thục, Archeveque de Huế* [sic], *Einsicht* (Special Edition), Una Voce-Gruppe Maria, Munich, August 1982, p 9

[6]   Idem, p 10

[7]   Idem, pp 9-10

[8]   Idem, p 9

[9]   Cf. Aloysius Pieris, op. cit., 2004, pp 256-257

[10]   Aloysius Pieris, op. cit., 2004, pp 256-257

[11]   Cf. Aloysius Pieris, op. cit., 2004, p 257

[12]   Cf. James S. Olson and Randy Roberts, *Where the Domino Fell:* 1991, p 55

[13]   Ngô-dinh-Thục, *'Misericordias Domini in Aeternum Cantabo':* 1982, p 9

[14]   idem, p 12

[15]   Aloysius Pieris, op. cit., 2004, pp 261-262

[16]   Idem, p 263

[17]   Walter Kasper, 'The whole truth is only found together,' *The Tablet,* London, 6th July 2002, p 4

18 Yves Congar, *Challenge to the Church: The Case of Archbishop Lefebvre [La Crise dans l'Eglise et Mgr Lefebvre],* Collins Liturgical Publications, London, 1978, p 35

19 Vincentii Lirinensis, *Commonitorium – Editio Nova,* Seguin, Avignon, 1821, p 12

20 Johann Adam Möhler, *Unity in the Church or the Principle of Catholicism,* Catholic University of America Press, Washington DC, 1996, pp 141-142

21 Idem, p 196

22 Ngô-dinh-Thục, *'Misericordias Domini in Aeternum Cantabo':* 1982, p 10

23 Bishop Donald J. Sanborn, Most Holy Trinity Seminary Newsletter, November 2017, p 2 http://mostholytrinityseminary.org/Nov_2017_ Newsletter.pdf [accessed 17th June 2018]

24 Ibid.

25 Ibid.

26 Archbishop Emmanuel Milingo (President), Archbishop George A. Stallings (Vice-President), Archbishop Peter P. Brennan (Vicar General), Archbishop Patrick E. Trujillo (Chancellor), Archbishop Joseph J. Gouthro (Secretary General), *re. Married Priests Now! Response to Corpus Statement,* 14th-16th February 2007 — http://www. renewedpriesthood.org/ca/page.cfm?Web_ID=892 [accessed 10th June 2018]

27 Ibid.

28 Karl Rahner, *The Shape of the Church to Come,* SPCK, London, 1974, p 111

29 Thomas J. Paprocki, 'Part V: The Method of Proceeding in Administrative Recourse and in the Removal or Transfer of Pastors (cc. 1732-1752),' in John P. Beal et al (eds), *New Commentary on the Code of Canon Law,* Paulist Press, New York / Mahwah NJ, 2000, [pp. 1818-47], p 1847

30 Ibid.

31 Ibid.

32 Johann Adam Möhler, *Unity in the Church,* pp 124-125

33 Idem, p 125

34 Idem, p 124

35 Richard P. McBrien, *Catholicism,* Geoffrey Chapman, London, 1994, p 3

36 Marcel Lefebvre, *An Open Letter to Confused Catholics,* Fowler Wright Books for The Society of St. Pius X, Leominster, 1986, p 145

37 Cf. John Thavis, *The Vatican Diaries,* Penguin, London, 2013, pp 7-8

38 Cf. Louis Billot, *Tractatus de Ecclesia Christi,* (third edition), Giachetti, Prato, 1909, pp 620-621

[39] John R. Quinn, *The Reform of The Papacy: The Costly Call to Christian Unity,* The Crossroad Publishing Company (Herder and Herder), New York, 1999, p 14

[40] Leo Joseph Cardinal Suenens, *The Tablet,* 17th May 1969, p 14

[41] *Einsicht,* Yr. 13, No. 1, May 1983, Una Voce Group, Munich, p 34

[42] Ibid.

[43] Cf. Richard P. McBrien, *Ministry: A Theological, Pastoral Handbook,* Harper & Row, San Francisco, 1988, pp 37-38 and pp 45-46

[44] Ibid.

[45] Cf. Frances D'Emilio, 'Vatican dismisses defiant archbishop from clergy,' 18th December 2009, http://www.boston.com/news/world/africa/articles/2009/12/18/vatican_defrocks_defiant_african_archbishop/?camp=pm [accessed 4 January 2015] and John L. Allen Jr., 'The last act in the Milingo story?', National Catholic Reporter, 17th December 2009, http://ncronline.org/blogs/ncr-today/last-act-milingo-story [accessed 4th October 2018]

[46] Arthur Michael Ramsey, *The Gospel and the Catholic Church,* Longmans, Green and Co., London, 1936, p 219

ACKNOWLEDGEMENTS

I am delighted to be able to offer a few words of thanks to those who have contributed in many and varied ways to the realization of this book. My interest in the topic dates way back to my days at the *Istituto Superiore di Scienze Religiose* under the great Rev. Prof. Nicola Tommasini, while I also learned much from working alongside the late Don Giovanni Mele (who since his passing has become known as 'The Priest of the Poor') and the late Archbishop Antonio Ciliberti who baptized and confirmed me — all great priests of a time gone by. Heartfelt thanks go out to my Godfather Don Angelo Tataranni, in whose company I hung out with stars and sedevacantists. In my subsequent studies at Trinity & All Saints, York St. John, and the Durham Center for Catholic Studies too, I was always fortunate to find great and inspiring teachers.

For this project especially I wish to thank Gloria Beaumont, Fr. Rory Geoghegan and Nicolás Tubaro for their priceless insights, Cathy Caridi, Rev. Dr Anthony Nguyen-dinh-Due, Prof. Edward N. Peters, Fr. Francis Tran-van-Dong and Prof. Luke Truong-tuan-An for invaluable pieces of advice and information. Many, many thanks to Maija Yang Institute of Education where I began the writing, to Chulalongkorn University, the Pontifical Gregorian University, Heythrop College, the Bodleian Library, the Maryknoll Archives, the Catholic Bishops' Conference of Vietnam, the Archdioceses of Huế and Ho-chi-Minh City and the Diocese of Vinh Long.

And all would be impossible without brilliant family and friends: for their ongoing encouragement I warmly thank Sr. Dr Margaret Atkins OSA and Dr Simon Bryden-Brook. Special thanks to Rev. Dr John R. Mabry and Apocryphile Press. Thanks a lot to Emily

Manis for reading and motivating, to Patricia Guitti Pollastri for her limitless optimism, and Rachanee Surintharat — a colorful blossom of Southeast Asia, and a natural spring of patience and help.

Edward Jarvis
Rangoon, Burma, 9th October 2018

SOURCES

ADAM, Karl, *The Spirit of Catholicism,* Sheed & Ward, London, 1934

AHERN, Thomas L. Jr., *CIA and the House of Ngô: Covert Action in South Vietnam, 1954-1963* (Unclassified), Center for the Study of Intelligence, Washington, 2000

ALLEN, John L. Jr., *The Future Church – How Ten Trends are Revolutionizing the Catholic Church,* Image, New York, 2009

ANSON, Peter F., *Bishops at Large,* Apocryphile Press, Berkeley CA, 2006

BARRETT, David V., *Sects, 'Cults' and Alternative Religions,* Blandford (a Cassell imprint), London, 1998

BARRIOS, Manuel and GARRIDO-CONDE, Maria-Teresa, *El Apasionante Misterio del Palmar de Troya [The Thrilling Mystery of El Palmar de Troya],* Editorial Planeta, Barcelona, 1977

BEAL, John P. et al (eds), *New Commentary on the Code of Canon Law,* Paulist Press, New York / Mahwah NJ, 2000:
PAPROCKI, Thomas J., 'Part V: The Method of Proceeding in Administrative Recourse and in the Removal or Transfer of Pastors (cc. 1732-1752),' [pp 1818-47]

BELL—see SCOTT, Peter

BERRIER, Hilaire du, *Background to Betrayal: The Tragedy of Vietnam,* Western Islands, Belmont MA, 1965

BURÓN—see GÓMEZ BURÓN, Joaquín

BILLOT, Louis, *Tractatus de Ecclesia Christi,* (third edition), Giachetti, Prato, 1909

CHANTIN, Jean-Pierre (ed), *Les Marges du Christianisme: "sectes", dissidences, ésotérisme; Dictionnaire du monde religeux dans la France contemporaine 10 [The Margins of Christianity: "sects", dissidences, esoterism; Dictionary of the religious world in contemporary France No. 10]*, Beauchesne, Paris, 2001

CONGAR, Yves, *Challenge to the Church: The Case of Archbishop Lefebvre [La Crise dans l'Eglise et Mgr Lefebvre]*, Collins Liturgical Publications, London, 1977

CUNEO, Michael W., *The Smoke of Satan*, Johns Hopkins University Press, Baltimore, Maryland 1999

DU BERRIER—see BERRIER

DULLES, Avery:
- *The Resilient Church*, Gill and Macmillan, Dublin, 1978
- *The Catholicity of The Church*, Clarendon Press, Oxford, 1987

GÓMEZ BURÓN, Joaquín and ALONSO, Antonio Martin, *El Enigma de El Palmar de Troya*, Editorial Personas, Barcelona, 1976

HALBERSTAM, David, *The Making of a Quagmire*, Random House, New York, 1965

HEBBLETHWAITE, Peter, *The Runaway Church*, Collins Fount, Glasgow, 1978

JACOBS, Seth, *America's Miracle Man in Vietnam: Ngo Dinh Diệm, Religion, Race, and U.S. Intervention in Southeast Asia*, Duke University Press, Durham NC, 2004

JARVIS, Edward, *God, Land and Freedom: The True Story of I.C.A.B.*, Apocryphile Press, Berkeley CA, 2018

KOMONCHAK—see WEAVER, Mary Jo

KEITH, Charles, *Catholic Vietnam: a Church from Empire to Nation*, University of California Press, Berkeley CA, 2012

KELLY, Clarence, *The Sacred and the Profane*, Seminary Press, Round Top NY, 1997

LAKELAND, Paul, *Church – Living Communion*, Liturgical Press, Collegeville MN, 2009

LANGGUTH, A.J., *Our Vietnam: The War 1954-1975*, Simon & Schuster, New York, 2000

LEFEBVRE, Marcel:
- *An Open Letter to Confused Catholics*, Fowler Wright Books for The Society of St. Pius X, Leominster, 1986
- *A Bishop Speaks – Writings and Addresses 1963-1975,* Scottish Una Voce, Edinburgh, 1979

LUNDBERG, Magnus, *A Pope of their Own: El Palmar de Troya and the Palmarian Church,* Uppsala Studies in Church History 1, Uppsala University, Department of Theology, 2017

MABRY—see PLUMMER, John P.

McBRIEN, Richard P.:
- *Catholicism,* Geoffrey Chapman, London, 1994
- *Ministry: A Theological, Pastoral Handbook,* Harper & Row, San Francisco, 1988

McLEOD, Hugh (ed), *History of Christianity Volume 9, World Christianities c. 1914 – c. 2000,* Cambridge University Press, Cambridge, 2006:
WALSH, Michael, 'The Religious Ferment of the Sixties,' [pp 304-322]

MÖHLER, Johann Adam, *Unity in the Church or the Principle of Catholicism,* Catholic University of America Press, Washington DC, 1996

OLSON, James S. and ROBERTS, Randy, *Where the Domino Fell: America and Vietnam 1945 to 1990,* St. Martin's Press, New York, 1991

PAPROCKI—see BEAL, John P. et al

PIERIS—see SCOTT, Peter

PLUMMER, John P., *The Many Paths Of The Independent Sacramental Movement,* Apocryphile Press, Berkeley, CA, 2006

PLUMMER, John P. and MABRY, John R., *Who Are The Independent Catholics?,* Apocryphile Press, Berkeley CA, 2006

PRÜTER, Karl, *Bishops Extraordinary,* Saint Willibrord Press, Highlandville MO, 1985

QUINN, John R., *The Reform of The Papacy: The Costly Call to Christian Unity,* The Crossroad Publishing Company (Herder and Herder), New York, 1999

RAHNER, Karl, *The Shape of the Church to Come,* SPCK, London, 1974

RAMSEY, Arthur Michael, *The Gospel and the Catholic Church,* Longmans, Green and Co., London, 1936

RATZINGER, Joseph, *Salt of the Earth,* Ignatius Press, San Francisco, 1997

RUSH, Ormond, *Still Interpreting Vatican II – Some Hermeneutical Principles,* Paulist Press, New York / Mahwah NJ, 2004

SALZA, John and SISCOE, Robert, *True or False Pope? Refuting Sedevacantism and Other Modern Errors,* St. Thomas Aquinas Seminary Editions, Winona MN, 2015

SCHREITER, Robert J., *The New Catholicity: Theology between the Global and the Local,* Orbis, Maryknoll NY, 1997

SCOTT, Peter and CAVANAUGH, William T. (eds), *The Blackwell Companion to Political Theology,* Blackwell, Oxford, 2004:
PIERIS, Aloysius, 'Political Theologies in Asia,' [pp 256-270]
BELL, Daniel M. Jr., 'State and Civil Society,' [pp 423-438]

SISCOE—see SALZA, John

THAVIS, John, *The Vatican Diaries,* Penguin, London, 2013

TØNNESSON, Stein, *The Vietnamese Revolution of 1945: Roosevelt, Ho Chi Minh and De Gaulle in a World at War,* (PRIO Monographs, Oslo), Sage Publications, London, 1991

TUCKER, Spencer C. (ed), *The Encyclopedia of the Vietnam War, a Political, Social, and Military History,* ABC-CLIO, Santa Barbara CA, 2011

VINCENT OF LERINS (Vincentii Lirinensis) *Commonitorium – Editio Nova,* Seguin, Avignon, 1821

WALSH—see McLEOD, Hugh

WEAVER, Mary Jo and APPLEBY, R. Scott (eds), *Being Right – Conservative Catholics in America,* Indiana University Press, Bloomington IN, 1995:
KOMONCHAK, Joseph A., 'Interpreting the Council – Catholic Attitudes toward Vatican II,' [pp 17-36]

YOUNG, Robert J.C., *Colonial Desire: Hybridity in Theory, Culture & Race,* Routledge, London, 1995

ARTICLES

ALLEN, John L. Jr., 'The last act in the Milingo story?', National Catholic Reporter, 17th December 2009, http://ncronline.org/blogs/ncr-today/last-act-milingo-story [accessed 4th October 2018]

BARBARA, Noel, 'The Episcopal Consecrations Conferred by His Excellency Archbishop Peter-Martin Ngo-dinh-Thục,' in Fortes in Fide No. 12, 1993, [pp 36-37]

CAPRILE, Giovanni, 'Su alcune illegittime Ordinazioni Sacerdotali ed Episcopali' [Regarding some illegitimate Priestly and Episcopal Ordinations], (Cronaca Contemporanea – Vita della Chiesa) in Civiltà Cattolica, Year 127, Vol. IV, No. 3034, 20th November 1976, [pp 375-378]

CEKADA, Anthony:
- (as 'Peregrinus'), 'Two Bishops in Every Garage,' The Roman Catholic, No. 12, Fall-Winter 1992, [pp 16-32] reproduced in KELLY, Clarence, The Sacred and The Profane, Seminary Press, Round Top NY, 1997, Appendix B [pp 287-319]
- 'Resisting the Pope, Sedevacantism and Frankenchurch: a short case for sedevacantism,' 2005 – http://www.traditional-mass.org/images/articles/Resist-Franken-P.pdf [accessed 6th June 2018], also published in The Remnant, November 2005
- 'The Validity of the Thục Consecrations,' [published in Spanish as 'La Validez de las Consagraciones de Monsenor Ngô-dinh-Thục'], Revista Integrismo, Buenos Aires, 2006 – http://www.traditionalmass.org/articles/article.php?id=60&catname=13 [accessed 12th June 2018]
- 'The Nine vs. Lefebvre – We Resist You to Your Face (2008): the story of our battle in court with Abp. Lefebvre and the Society of St. Pius X,' at www.traditionalmass.org – http://www.traditionalmass.org/images/articles/NineVLefebvre.pdf [accessed 10th June 2018]

CONGREGATION FOR THE DOCTRINE OF THE FAITH (CDF), 12th March 1983, L'Osservatore Romano, English Edition, 18th April 1983

D'EMILIO—see EMILIO, Frances D'

DERKSEN, Mario, 'An Open Letter to Bishop Clarence Kelly on the "Thục Bishops" and the errors in The Sacred and the Profane,' Cincinnati OH, 8th January 2011, www.thucbishops.com [accessed 6th June 2018]

DES LAURIERS—see LAURIERS

'DOMINICUS,' 'Petit Catéchisme du Sédévacantisme' [Short Catechism of Sedevacantism], Le Sel de La Terre, No. 79, Winter 2011-2012, [pp 36-47]

EINSICHT, published by Una-Voce-Gruppe Maria, Munich. Selected editions:

- August 1982 (Special Edition): Ngô-dinh-Thục, '"Misericordias Domini in Aeternum Cantabo": Autobiographie de Mgr. Pierre Martin Ngô-dinh-Thục, Archeveque de Huế' [sic]; May 1983, No. 1, Year 13; February 1985, No. 6, Year 14; April 1998 /2 (Special Edition), Year 28: Ngô-dinh-Thục, 'Declaration'

EMILIO, Frances D', 'Vatican dismisses defiant archbishop from clergy,' 18th December 2009, http://www.boston.com/news/world/africa/articles/2009/12/18/vatican_defrocks_defiant_african_archbishop/?camp=pm [accessed 4 January 2015]

HOSKINS, Janet Alison, 'An Unjealous God? Christian Elements in a Vietnamese Syncretistic Religion,' Current Anthropology, Vol. 55, No. S10, 1st December 2014 (volume supplement), p S302

KASPER, Walter, 'The whole truth is only found together,' The Tablet, London, 6th July 2002

LAURIERS, Guérard des, (interview with), Sodalitium (Spanish edition) No. 13, March 1988

MILINGO, Emmanuel et al, 'Married Priests Now! Response to Corpus Statement,' 14th-16th February 2007 — http://www.renewedpriesthood.org/ca/page.cfm?Web_ID=892 [accessed 10th June 2018]

PUSKORIUS, Casimir, 'Non Habemus Papam (On the Election of Benedict XVI)' at http://www.cmri.org/02-non-habemus-papem.shtml [accessed 6th June 2018]

SANBORN, Donald J., Most Holy Trinity Seminary Newsletter, November 2017, http://mostholytrinityseminary.org/Nov_2017_Newsletter.pdf [accessed 17th June 2018]

SHAPLEN, Robert, 'Nine Years after a Fateful Assassination,' New York Times, 14th May 1972, p 16

SUENENS, Leo Joseph, (Letter), The Tablet, 17th May 1969, p 14

TIME, 1st May 1964, quoted in Hilaire du Berrier, Background to Betrayal: 1965, p 147

TUAN HOANG, 'The Last Years of Ngô-dình-Thục' – www.tu-
    annyriver.com – https://tuannyriver.com/2017/08/21/the-last-
    years-of-ngo-dinh-thuc/ [accessed 10th June 2018]
See also:
ACTA SYNODALIA Sacrosancti Concilii Oecumenici Vaticani II,
    Vol. II, Part I
ACTA SYNODALIA Sacrosancti Concilii Oecumenici Vaticani II,
    Vol. II, Part III

ABOUT THE AUTHOR

Edward Jarvis was born in Yorkshire, England, in 1975. He studied philosophy, theology, and religious studies, first in Italy and then in England. He graduated top of his Department in 2004 and went on to take advanced degrees and conduct postgraduate research. He is fluent in several languages and currently teaches and writes in Southeast Asia.

YOU MAY ALSO ENJOY

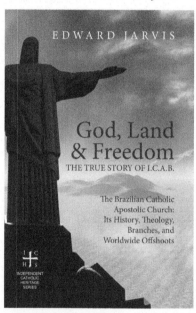

Two decades before the Second Vatican Council, a section of the Catholic Church decided to enact sweeping reforms of its own. The Brazilian Catholic Apostolic Church, or I.C.A.B., abolished latin, celibacy and confession, embraced religious freedom, and redefined the pope as just another bishop. *God, Land and Freedom, The True Story of I.C.A.B.*, tells this remarkable story as it has never been told before.

ISBN 978-1-947826-90-8 | paperback $18.95